TAROT
Get the Whole Story

About the Author

James Ricklef, a certified Tarot master, is a former member of the board of directors of the American Tarot Association, and for many years he has been a featured speaker at the annual Los Angeles Tarot Symposium. He also is a freelance writer, and his Tarot articles, including his "Ask KnightHawk" column, have been published in many Tarot newsletters and magazines. In addition, he teaches classes on how to read Tarot cards and how to use them in other ways for personal empowerment.

TAROT
Get the Whole Story

Use, Create & Interpret
Tarot Spreads

James Ricklef

Llewellyn Publications
St. Paul, Minnesota

First Edition
First Printing, 2004

Book design and editing by Joanna Willis
Card from the *Universal Tarot* by Roberto de Angelis © 2000 by Lo Scarabeo and reprinted with permission from Lo Scarabeo
Cards from *The Robin Wood Tarot* by Robin Wood and *The World Spirit Tarot* by Lauren O'Leary © Llewellyn Worldwide
Cover design by Lisa Novak
Cover image © 2004 by Leo Tushaus, using cards from *The Gilded Tarot* by Ciro Marchetti © Llewellyn Worldwide

Library of Congress Cataloging-in-Publication Data
Ricklef, James, 1954–
    Tarot: get the whole story: use, create & interpret tarot spreads / James Ricklef.—1st ed.
      p.   cm.
    Includes bibliographical references.
    ISBN 0-7387-0345-1
    1. Tarot. I. Title.

BF1879.T2R52 2004
133.3'2424—dc22

2004048955

Llewellyn Worldwide does not participate in, endorse, or have any authority or responsibility concerning private business transactions between our authors and the public.

    All mail addressed to the author is forwarded but the publisher cannot, unless specifically instructed by the author, give out an address or phone number.

    Any Internet references contained in this work are current at publication time, but the publisher cannot guarantee that a specific location will continue to be maintained. Please refer to the publisher's website for links to authors' websites and other sources.

Llewellyn Publications
A Division of Llewellyn Worldwide, Ltd.
P.O. Box 64383, Dept. 0-7387-0345-1
St. Paul, MN 55164-0383, U.S.A.
www.llewellyn.com

 Printed in the United States of America on recycled paper

To Wil,
whose love and support continue to enrich and enchant my life.

Also by James Ricklef

KnightHawk's Tarot Readings
(Writers Club Press)

Tarot Tells the Tale
(Llewellyn Publications)

Contents

Illustrations

Introduction

The most common way to do a Tarot reading involves the use of a spread. A spread is a predetermined design for laying out a given number of cards. Each position in the layout is assigned a meaning, and the card dealt into it is interpreted in the context of that positional meaning. Thus, for example, the message of a card dealt into a position called "The obstacle" would be very different from the message for the same card when dealt into a position called "Advice."

Besides influencing the interpretation of the individual cards, a spread facilitates the discovery of a unified message for a reading. It provides the structure upon which the threads of the individual card meanings are woven into a tapestry that tells a story. In addition, the matrix of cards that a spread defines implies a set of interrelationships between those cards. These relationships reveal additional nuances about each card, synergistically augmenting the message of each card and of the reading in general.

There are several spreads, such as the three-card Past, Present, Future spread and the ten-card Celtic Cross spread, that are so well known and widely used that practically every Tarot reader knows of them. In addition, however, there are hundreds of other spreads in common usage, many of which are described in one Tarot book or another.

Where, then, do all of these Tarot spreads come from? Are they handed down from some arcane source, or is it the concern and responsibility of a select few Tarot adepts to devise them? Actually, they evolve within the entire Tarot community. While it is true that some Tarot spreads were created by recognized Tarot experts, many of them developed naturally through popular usage over the years, spreading and evolving by word of mouth. Along the way, though, some of these spreads have been published by one Tarot authority or another. An example of this is the almost ubiquitous Celtic Cross spread, which, in 1910, A. E. Waite included in his book *The Pictorial Key to the Tarot*. Waite presented a brief description of this spread without claiming to have created it himself, and the common assumption is that variations of it had been used for many years before Waite recorded it.[1]

While there is value in learning the tried and true in any art form, we are not restricted to using only those spreads that have been written down somewhere or that have been taught to us by an acknowledged authority. In addition to being developed by Tarot experts or evolving within the Tarot community, a spread may spring from the heart and soul of any Tarot reader. Anyone can create a spread. The only limit to the number and variety of Tarot spreads available to us lies within the bounds of our collective imagination.

The art of creating a Tarot spread is easy to learn, although the actual process can be as easy or as complex as the spread we want to create. This book will describe and demonstrate that process in detail for you.

Tarot students often wonder if a spread that they make up can be as valid as an established one. The answer, of course, is that it can be. No matter what spread we use—whether it is one we have created or an established one we have learned somewhere—the most important factors contributing to a successful reading with it are the depth of our understanding of that spread and our sincere intention to use it.[2] Consequently, a spread we create may work even better than one we learn from a book since we have invested a part of ourselves in it and we probably understand it better than one created by someone else.

Sooner or later you will be ready to create your own spreads, and the concepts presented and demonstrated in this book should encourage and enable you to do so. In the meantime, however, the primary intention of this book is to present and illustrate the use of some valuable Tarot spreads that are applicable to a wide range of situations.

---

1. The details of the definition and use of this spread are different in practically every book in which I have seen it described. This is a testament to the fact that even to this day, the Celtic Cross is a flexible and adaptable entity, alive within the Tarot culture.

2. Some people believe that our subconscious mind chooses the cards for a reading. Some say it is our soul or higher self, and others think it is a divine agency such as the spirit of the universe. In any case, it is important that once we choose a spread to use, we then communicate that choice via our intention to whatever that agency may be so that it can communicate effectively back to us using the structure of the chosen spread.

Some of the spreads described in this book are loosely based on traditional ones within the extant Tarot folklore, but others have been created from scratch, inspired by a variety of disparate sources. In either case, the spreads in this book are useful in addressing issues such as finding or healing a relationship, overcoming specific problems, dealing with pain and sorrow, looking for the timing of future events, gaining a deeper understanding of a perplexing situation, and transforming your life. In short, there is a spread in this book for almost any Tarot reading.

Each spread will be explained in great detail. The process by which it was created will be discussed, which will demonstrate how you can design your own spreads. The structure, meaning, and use of each spread will be illustrated through an entertaining sample reading, which also will be explained in detail. In addition, alternative spreads, which are variations of the ones illustrated, will be presented and explained.

Before we delve into these spreads, however, chapter 1 will introduce techniques that are useful in the creation of Tarot spreads. It will suggest where to find inspiration for them, how to define their positional meanings, and how to structure the layout of their cards. It also will discuss how existing spreads can be personalized and modified to meet your particular needs.

ONE
How to Create Spreads

There are hundreds of spreads documented in the body of Tarot literature from which we may choose to do a reading, but sometimes we may want to create one of our own, either for one particular reading or to be used repeatedly for a general type of reading. In either case, there are various reasons for creating a Tarot spread. Perhaps the querent, topic, or question for a reading has specific needs that call for an individualized spread. Maybe we want a spread that suits our own distinctive style of reading Tarot cards or one that satisfies our individual philosophical outlook. Of course, there is also great personal value in using a spread whose meaning springs from our own mind and soul and in which we have invested our own energy.

In any case, if we want to create a spread, there are many different ways to do so. Indeed, this is a topic that could fill a book, but it is beyond the scope of this one to provide such an extensive coverage of it. What follows, though, is an introduction to some of the easier and more common techniques for creating Tarot spreads, along with some illustrative examples of them.

Problem Solving

Sometimes a specific problem calls for a specially designed spread. An effective way to create such a spread is to begin by discussing the problem with the querent in order to discern the issues that underlie, comprise, or border upon the stated problem. Next, define card positions for the spread based on the issues or questions that result from that discussion. Flexibility in doing so is advisable, since some of the issues may overlap enough that they can be combined into one spread position, or one issue may be extensive enough that it should be broken down into two or more positions. This is, of course, an intuitive process, and if the querent is amenable to participating in it, then a reading with the resulting spread will have all the more relevance to him or her.

Once the list of card positions is finalized, a meaningful pattern for the cards must be determined. This step is a very personal one, since it depends to a great extent upon the individualized concepts and meanings that you associate with various shapes, patterns, and directions. For example, you may associate a straight line with progression or the flow of time, a triangle with divinity, a square with stability and order, a circle with cycles, and a star with spiritual aspirations. You might want to put guidance cards above other cards, cards dealing with the past on the left, and future cards on the right. It may seem most reasonable to place cards about unconscious or underlying issues below other cards, and ones about the basic or central issue in the middle of the spread.

While associations such as the ones noted above may be suggested or recommended by some external authority such as a teacher or a text, you are the final arbiter of what works for you. You may have entirely different concepts about such associations, so use whatever makes sense to you. Throughout this chapter and the next one I have illustrated many of my own techniques for designing card layouts, but my ideas should be taken as suggestions, not mandates.

As an example of creating a spread to solve a specific problem, let's look at the process by which I designed one to help a querent find success in an endeavor he was about to undertake. As the querent and I discussed his proposed enterprise, a few points came up that we thought the reading should address. For one thing, he wished that he knew more about what he was getting into. We broke this issue down into two positions: "The main thing you need to know" and "Underlying factors." In addition, he wondered what obstacles he should prepare for, and I suggested that he also might want to know what assistance may be available to him. Finally, we decided that it would be helpful to know what he could do to improve his chances of success.

This discussion led us to create five positions for the reading, which we decided to arrange in the pattern of a four-pointed diamond with one card in the center. There were other shapes that suggested themselves as well, such as a five-pointed star and a square with one card inside it, but we thought a diamond represented material success, which was what the querent sought. Thus, we arrived at the layout shown in Figure 1.

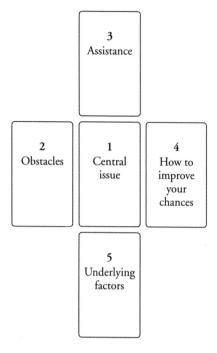

Figure 1. The Success spread.

The following describes the resulting position definitions and the rationale behind their arrangement:

1. What is the main thing you need to know about the endeavor you are facing?
   (I put this card in the middle since it is the central issue.)

2. What is working against you as you enter into this endeavor?
   (I put this card behind card 1 because it is what pulls you back.)

3. What can help you?
   (Since this card represents assistance, I placed it above card 1.)

4. What can you do to improve your chances of success?
   (I put this card in front of card 1 because it is what pulls you forward.)

5. What underlying factors about this endeavor should you be aware of?
   (This card represents hidden factors that are coming in under the radar or that are the foundation underlying the central issue so I put it under card 1.)

Note that while this spread was created for one particular reading, it may be suitable for any reading that calls for advice on how to succeed at something. In fact, it is often the case that a spread created for one particular reading turns out to have general applicability, which is something that should be kept in mind while using any of the techniques presented in this chapter.

Inspiration from a Shape

Instead of creating the shape of a layout based on the intent of the spread (as seen in the previous section), a spread may be created by first considering an interesting shape and then defining card positions based on the theme suggested by that shape. Abstract shapes such as a triangle, a square, a star, or a cross can be used for this purpose, but I have had better results using more concrete shapes, such as the human body or a tree.[3] Of course, in that case, the layout pattern will be a stylized representation of the shape.

In the following example, I began by thinking of a tree and several of its main components, such as roots, trunk, bark, branches, and leaves. The card layout that I designed based on these considerations is illustrated in Figure 2.

With this layout in mind, I then created the following positional meanings based on concepts that I associated with the five components that I chose to use.

1. What keeps you grounded?
   (Roots)

2. What supports you?
   (Trunk)

3. What protects you?
   (Bark)

---

3. In a workshop taught by Mary Greer and Rachel Pollack, I saw some great examples of this technique. Pollack demonstrated the Tarot of the Body spread (which was developed by Anita Jensen), and Greer demonstrated the Hanged Man spread, which is also described in her book *The Complete Book of Tarot Reversals* (220–22).

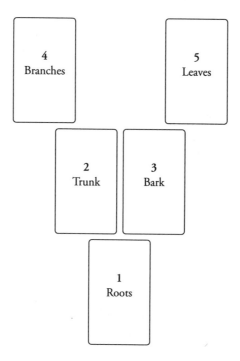

Figure 2. The Tree spread.

4. What are you reaching out for?
   (*Branches*)

5. What nourishes you?
   (*Leaves*)

Of course, these associations are my own. Beginning with the same design, you might come up with very different positional meanings.

As an exercise of your own, try creating a spread based on the following components of the human body: head, heart, guts, left arm, right arm, left leg, and right leg. To help you with this process, you might want to consider some common attributes associated with the right and left. Traditionally, the right is associated with things like giving, masculinity, activity, offense, science, conservative views, and approval, while the left traditionally has been associated with receiving, femininity, passivity, defense, magic, liberal views, and condemnation.

Dealing Cards for Questions

Another way that you can create a spread based on a given shape is to deal cards into the chosen pattern and define the positions based on your interpretation of those cards.[4] In this case, an abstract shape works well if it implies a meaning that is relevant to the intent of the spread. That intent also sets the tone for the process of defining the positional meanings based on the cards dealt. Once the spread's layout and positional definitions have been set, those cards are shuffled back into the deck and new cards should be dealt in order to do the reading itself.[5]

To illustrate this technique, I shall describe the process I once used to create a spread to help a querent overcome marital problems. For the shape of the spread, I first considered that an upward-pointing triangle traditionally represents the masculine principle, and a downward-pointing triangle represents the feminine. If we overlay those two symbols (i.e., marry them together), we get the six-pointed Star of David, which yields six positions—one for each point of the star. In addition, though, I felt there also should be one card in the center of the layout to represent the marriage itself as the union of both people, which makes this a seven-card spread. I then dealt seven cards to get the spread illustrated in Figure 3.

The following are the cards that I dealt and the positional meanings I saw in them.

1. Ace of Wands: How can you be more creative with your marriage?

2. Temperance: Where does your relationship need more balance or moderation?

3. Ten of Wands: In what ways do you feel burdened by your marriage?

4. The Hanged Man: What aspect of your marriage do you need to see from a different point of view?

5. Three of Wands: What is your vision for your marriage? In other words, where do you see it going from here?

---

4. This technique was inspired by an exercise in a workshop taught by Mary Greer and Rachel Pollack in which we drew several major arcana cards to pose questions, then dealt cards to answer those questions.

5. Alternatively, cards from one deck may be used for defining the spread positions, while another deck may be used for the reading itself.

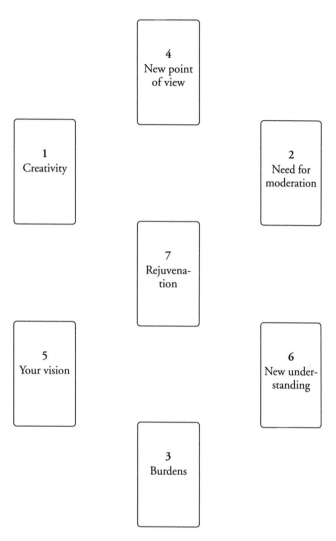

Figure 3. The Relationship Rejuvenation spread.

6. Page of Swords: What new and unexpected things are you just now learning about your spouse and about your marriage itself?

7. Judgement: How can you rejuvenate and revitalize your marriage?

Note that I did not use reversed cards for this technique, although that does not mean they cannot be used. Also, it is important to reiterate here that the cards indicated above were used for defining the layout positions only. New cards were dealt to do the actual reading.

Modification of an Existing Spread

We can create a new spread based upon an old one by modifying it in any of several ways, including expanding it, contracting it, redefining its positions, or merging it with another spread. First, let's see how we can enlarge one spread in order to create a new one.

One way that an existing spread can be expanded is by taking its card positions and breaking some of them into two or more component pieces. For example, in the three-card Past, Present, Future spread, we can convert the first position into two new positions, "Distant past" and "Recent past," while the "Future" position can be expanded into "Near future" and "Probable final outcome."[6] The "Present" can be broken down into three positions, where the first one deals with the current situation in general, the second one illustrates what the querent thinks is happening, and the third shows what the querent is unaware of in the current situation. With these changes, we have converted the familiar Past, Present, Future spread into the seven-card spread illustrated in Figure 4.

Another technique for expanding a spread is to create new positions that develop it along a logical progression from the original spread or that take it on an interesting tangent. As an example of a logical progression, the three-card Background, Problem, Advice spread may become a four-card spread by adding a card for the probable outcome if the querent follows the offered advice. We may develop it further by adding another card for the probable outcome if the querent ignores this advice, thus yielding the spread illustrated in Figure 5.

As an example of taking a spread on an interesting tangent, consider again the Background, Problem, Advice spread. The first card deals with the background of the querent's problem, but we also might want to explore a similar problem that the querent has faced in the past, how well she or he handled it, and how it could have been resolved more effectively. Adding cards to handle these three points leads us to the spread in Figure 6.

Going in the opposite direction, some large spreads have embedded within them subspreads that can be more effective in some situations, especially when either time or the

---

6. See the section "The Extended Temporal Spread: A Five-Card Spread" in chapter 2 for a sample reading using this spread.

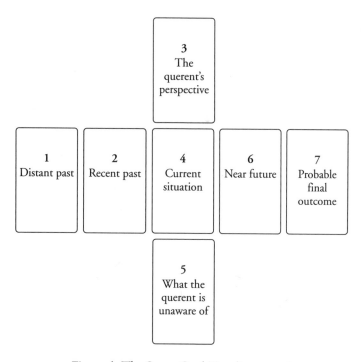

Figure 4. The Seven-Card Timeline spread.

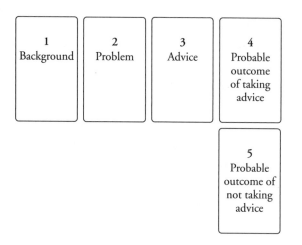

Figure 5. The Advice and Outcome spread.

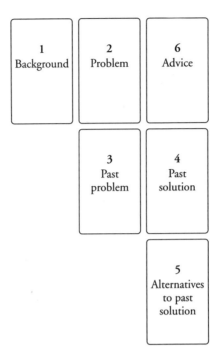

Figure 6. The Problems and Solutions spread.

scope of the reading needs to be limited. For example, if a reading with the ten-card Celtic Cross spread is expected to run longer than time allows, we may prefer to use its first six cards (the cross) but not the final four cards (the staff). In fact, this abbreviated version of the Celtic Cross formed the basis of the spread described in "The Modified Celtic Cross Relationship Spread: A Six-Card Spread" in chapter 2.

Sometimes the basic layout of a spread is suitable, but the positional definitions are not specific or relevant enough for the situation. In that case, we can redefine the positions. For example, if we are doing a relationship reading in which the querent has had a fight with his or her partner, the Background, Problem, Advice spread may be redefined to be more specifically suited to the situation, as with the following positional definitions:

1. What factors have contributed to the recent conflict in your relationship?

2. What do you need to understand about your role in this conflict?

3. How can you restore peace in your relationship?

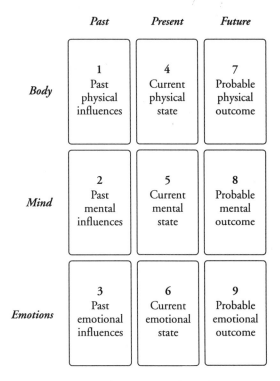

	Past	Present	Future
Body	**1** Past physical influences	**4** Current physical state	**7** Probable physical outcome
Mind	**2** Past mental influences	**5** Current mental state	**8** Probable mental outcome
Emotions	**3** Past emotional influences	**6** Current emotional state	**9** Probable emotional outcome

Figure 7. The Journey Through Time spread.

Another technique for modifying existing spreads is to combine two or more of them into one larger spread. One way of doing this is to insert the positions of one spread into the layout of another one, especially when the two spreads are somewhat related. An example of this is the spread described in "The Expanded Choice Spread: An Eight-Card Spread" in chapter 2.

Alternatively, we can blend or merge the positions of two very different spreads in order to create a new spread that is a hybrid of the original ones. As an example of this, consider two three-card spreads: Body, Mind, Emotions and Past, Present, Future. From these two spreads we can create a matrix that defines a nine-card spread as illustrated in Figure 7.

Inspiration from Another Source or System

While existing spreads provide a rich source of inspiration for new ones, almost anything that moves us or has meaning for us can form the basis of a new spread. Some of the most fruitful sources from which new spreads may spring include philosophical systems, religions of the world, or mythic tales. The possibilities here are endless, so the following list of suggestions is only the tip of the iceberg and is merely meant to illustrate the process and provide encouragement for your own exploration.

The number three has special significance in most religions, and three-card spreads may be created based on the significance of many divine triads. For example, Hinduism's Brahma, Vishnu, and Shiva might lead to this spread:

1. What kind of life are you creating at this time?

2. What aspect of your life needs protection?

3. What needs to be destroyed or eliminated from your life?

A few other divine triads that might inspire a Tarot spread are:

- Maiden, Mother, Crone

- Father, Son, Holy Ghost

- Isis, Osiris, Horus

- Zeus, Poseidon, Hades

In addition to triple aspects of divinity, the number three often comes up in spiritual teachings, such as the three pillars of the Qabalistic Tree of Life (mercy, balance, and severity). As an example of using a triad from a spiritual teaching, we might use the three Taoist principles of simplicity, patience, and compassion to create the following spread:

1. What should you simplify in your life?

2. With whom or what should you have more patience?

3. Where in your life do you need to exhibit more compassion?

The number four is often found in classification systems, like the four elements of alchemy (fire, water, air, and earth), the four seasons, and the four directions. Since many esoteric systems assign meanings to such quartets, they form the basis of many four-card spreads. For example, the four classical elements can have the following associations:

- Fire: spirit, vitality, and inspiration
- Water: emotions, intuition, and relationships
- Air: thought, ideas, and beliefs
- Earth: physical or material manifestations

This might lead us to the following spread:

1. What do you have a passion to do?

2. How do you feel about that activity?

3. What are your beliefs concerning it?

4. What tangible results might it yield?

Another example of a meaningful quartet can be found in the Buddhist teaching of four practices that are meant to heal us and the world around us:

- Loving kindness
- Compassionate understanding
- Sympathetic joy
- Equanimity

These four practices can be translated into a spread that is useful for meditative self-readings, although it can be used for readings for other people if they are seeking spiritual guidance. The following is a suggested spread using this philosophy:

1. How can I best express kindness toward others (or myself) in a loving way?

2. With whom do I need to find more compassion and empathy, and how might I do so?

3. What joy is someone else in my life experiencing that I can share and support?

4. How can I find peace and composure within a world of suffering?

In fact, there are many lists of principles, rules, and guidelines in Buddhism that can provide inspiration for spreads. For example:

- The Buddha's threefold body: essence, potentiality, and manifestation.

- The five faculties of power: faith, will, reliable memory, concentration, and wisdom.

- The six practices for reaching enlightenment: offering, morality, patience, endeavoring, concentration, and right judgment.

- The noble eightfold path: right view, right thought, right speech, right behavior, right livelihood, right effort, right mindfulness, and right concentration.

Some other sources of ideas for spreads include the seven planets of classical cosmology, the seven chakras of the human body, the eight trigrams of the I Ching (we could create a spread based on the I Ching's sixty-four hexagrams too, but that might be unwieldy), the ten sephiroth of the Qabalistic Tree of Life (for an example of this process, see "The Tree of Life Spread: A Ten-Card Spread" in chapter 2), the twelve signs of the zodiac, Odin's eighteen runes, and mythological pantheons such as that of the ancient Egyptians, Greeks, Celts, or Scandinavians. Inspiration for a spread even may be found in such diverse sources as the identifying characteristics of the knights of King Arthur's Round Table or the Beatitudes from Christ's Sermon on the Mount. In fact, I once helped a *Lord of the Rings* fan create a spread based on the predominant characteristics of various types of individuals in Tolkien's Middle Earth: hobbits, dwarves, men, elves, and wizards.

As the above discussion demonstrates, concepts from religious, spiritual, or philosophical systems are a vast source of ideas for a Tarot spread. Similarly, we can adapt ideas from any thought-provoking literary or artistic source, such as a quote, a magazine article, a play, a painting, or a book. Using such sources may take a bit more effort, though, because the philosophical sources noted above are already partitioned conveniently into discrete units, such as four elements, seven planets, or twelve astrological signs. The parsing of a quote into meaningful elements, on the other hand, requires some careful consideration. Yet once we have decided which of the basic concepts of our source to use, we can create a spread with one position per idea. For examples of how to use this technique, see the following sections in chapter 2 wherein spreads are created based on a quote, a picture, and a magazine article, respectively:

- "The Sorrow's Alchemy Spread: A Four-Card Spread"

- "The Lovers Card Spread: A Nine-Card Spread"

- "The Failure's Alchemy Spread: A Nine-Card Spread"

While the above techniques can help you create spreads tailored to your own individual requirements, philosophy, and style of reading the cards, they also provide a foundation for understanding the process by which the spreads in the next section were developed. So now let us shift our primary focus from creating spreads to using them as we examine a variety of spreads that are effective in many different situations. Keep in mind, however, that although you certainly can use these spreads as described, you also can modify them to suit your particular needs or just let them inspire you to create your own spreads.

TWO

Spreads and Readings

The sections in this chapter present, explain, and illustrate the use of a variety of Tarot spreads. These spreads are useful in a wide range of circumstances, some being geared toward specific types of readings such as romance or career, while others are more general in their application.

Each section begins with comments on the philosophy underlying the spread that it features, and it discusses the process by which that spread was created. If the spread is a modification of a traditional one, the section notes how and why it was altered. If it is entirely original, its inspiration and genesis are discussed. Hopefully, such discussions will inspire and enable you to create your own spreads as well.

Next, each section presents the card layout for the spread and the associated list of the positional meanings, followed by a sample reading using the spread. This reading illustrates the use of the spread—from the interpretation of the cards within the context of their layout positions to the subtleties of intercard relationships.

The "Ask KnightHawk" readings that illustrate the use of these spreads are sort of like "Dear Abby" columns using Tarot readings. (I have carried over the name KnightHawk here from my "Ask KnightHawk" column, which was first introduced in the online ATA [American Tarot Association] newsletter in October 1999.) All of these readings were done for well-known fictional or mythical characters or for historical figures. Being about familiar people and situations, they should be easy to follow and understand. It is important to note, however, that the readings in this book were performed as if they were actual Tarot readings. With the querent's question in mind, I shuffled and dealt the cards, and then interpreted the resulting spread. Of course, there are obvious differences between doing these readings and doing face-to-face readings for real people. For one thing, I could not have a dialogue with my fictional querents, which is something I try to do during readings in person. I like to make in-person readings as much of a cooperative venture between the querent and me as possible. Another difference is that there is no telling how much my a priori knowledge of the outcome for these querents influenced my understanding of the messages of the cards, although I endeavored to perform these readings without the benefit of such hindsight.

That consideration aside, the process of doing these readings was sometimes challenging, often illuminating, and always fascinating. For example, some of the cards in these readings communicated meanings that seemed obvious, while others required more time, effort, and patience to interpret. The obvious ones often conveyed a sense of wonder and awe as I marveled at how incredibly appropriate they were. For example, seeing the Hanged Man come up in the reading for Judas Iscariot sent a shiver up my spine (see "The Personal Transformation Spread: A Six-Card Spread").

However, the cards that were more difficult to understand generally provided the most value—for me, for the reading itself, and (hopefully) for you, the reader. For me, these difficult cards honed my skills as a Tarot reader and they renewed my appreciation for the depth and complexity of the Tarot cards. For the reading itself, such cards carried the reading beyond the predictable and into an exciting realm of enchantment and mystery. In fact, sometimes these cards revealed unexpected insights into the stories that provided the context for the readings. For you, the reader, the benefit of these perplexing cards lies in seeing how the difficulties of interpreting them can be overcome, which may give you ideas about how to handle such problems in your own Tarot readings. Hopefully, these cards will also imbue the readings in this book with added interest through the wonder and surprise that their unexpected insights bring.

After the sample reading, each section provides a commentary about it. These comments include remarks about the reading itself, specific notes regarding each position in the spread, and general notes about the spread as a whole.

Finally, alternative spreads are provided. In some cases, these are modified versions of the spread that is used in the section's reading. In other cases, the alternative spreads are related thematically or philosophically to the one that is the section's primary focus. Unfortunately, due to space limitations, it was not feasible to provide sample readings for these additional spreads. However, the insights provided by the readings for the main spread in each section should be applicable to these alternatives as well.

Before we consider these spreads, however, some observations about reading reversed cards are in order since the sample readings in this book include both upright and reversed cards.

Reversed cards come up in a reading when some cards get turned upside down during the shuffling process, either intentionally or unintentionally. Some people ignore reversals by merely turning any reversed cards back to their upright orientation, but many Tarot readers interpret a card differently when it is reversed than when it is upright. An exhaustive examination of how to do so is beyond the scope of this book, so what follows is only a brief explanation of how I work with reversals.[7]

I generally consider that when a card is reversed, its meaning or energy is being affected, afflicted, or mitigated in some way. A common interpretation of a reversal is that it indicates some sort of blockage of the card's meaning. This can be internal resistance on the querent's part, or it can signify that something in the querent's environment is blocking the manifestation of the card's meaning. Alternatively, its energy may be diminished (especially when the card is in a "Past" position) or it may be delayed (especially when the card is in a "Future" position). The message of the card may be hidden in that the querent may not be aware of it consciously, may be in denial about it, or may be projecting it on to someone else (especially for court cards).

A reversal may relate to internal aspects of the querent's life rather than to the external world, or it may be about extremes, such as there being too much of the card's energy (which may be a warning that the querent should release or move away from something) or too little (which may recommend that the querent strive to attain this card's quality). We also might look for an unusual or unexpected interpretation of a card when it is reversed. For example, if we typically consider the Seven of Cups to be about imagination, illusions, or confusion, then we might see it as an indication of healthy curiosity when it is reversed. Finally, sometimes it can be insightful just to examine the image on the card in its reversed orientation in order to see what the upside-down imagery brings to mind.

---

7. For a more in-depth look at how I handle reversed cards, see my book *Tarot Tells the Tale,* published by Llewellyn in 2003. Alternatively, an excellent book that covers this topic extensively is Mary Greer's *The Complete Book of Tarot Reversals,* published by Llewellyn in 2002.

The choice of which method to use is an intuitive one, although it depends on some objective factors such as the card's position in the spread, the question for the reading, the querent's reactions to the card, and the messages of adjacent cards in the spread. By learning these general techniques and keeping them in the back of your mind, your intuition will have them available so that it can offer an interpretation based on one or more of them.

While the methods noted above are some suggested ways of handling reversals, there are many others that people commonly use. How to interpret reversed cards is a personal choice, though, and there really is no right or wrong way—just a way that works for you. However, keeping the above techniques in mind should help you understand the readings in the following sections whenever a reversed card arises. In addition, seeing how the reversals in these readings are handled hopefully will illuminate the process of interpreting reversed cards.

THE DECISION SPREAD
A Three-Card Spread

Some people consider three-card spreads to be trivial, preferring instead to use spreads with significantly more cards. However, the depth of a reading is not limited by the number of cards in the spread, but by the experience and intention of the Tarot reader. Even if we only use three-card spreads for brief readings, there are times when such brevity is appropriate. For example, readings at a party or impromptu readings for friends usually are limited to a few minutes. Also, a short three-card reading can clarify an issue or point out where attention needs to be focused, thereby serving as either a prelude or an epilogue to a long reading with a more complex spread.

Regardless of the reason for using a three-card spread, there are many different types of them, some of which are described at the end of this section.[8] For this section's reading, I chose to use one called the Decision spread, which considers the pros and cons of an option that the querent is considering in order to help him or her decide a course of action.[9]

---

8. For a more detailed discussion of three-card spreads, as well as twenty-two sample readings with a wide variety of them, see my book *Tarot Tells the Tale.*

9. This reading is loosely based on a group effort from a workshop that I facilitated at the Los Angeles Tarot Symposium in June 2001. I would like to preface it with my thanks to all the people at that workshop for their enthusiastic participation.

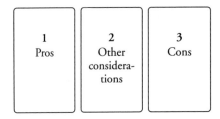

Figure 8. The Decision spread.

The Spread

Begin by dealing three cards as indicated in Figure 8.

Interpret these cards using the following positional meanings:

1. **Pros.** The advantages of the option being considered.

2. **Other considerations.** Considerations that may help the querent decide whether or not to take this action.

3. **Cons.** The disadvantages of the option being considered.

A KnightHawk Reading with the Decision Spread

Dear KnightHawk,

The studio is insisting that I star in Gone with the Wind, *but I don't want to do it. I'm afraid I won't live up to the public's concept of Rhett Butler. Besides that, I hate Cukor, the director, and I refuse to try to speak with a Southern accent. But Mayer is pressuring me to do this picture. What should I do?*

Sincerely,
Clark Gable

*   *   *

Dear Mr. Gable,

Thank you for asking me to do a Tarot reading to help you with this big decision. Rather than do a reading to tell you what to do, however, I think it will be of greater value for you to see what the Tarot has to say about the advantages and disadvantages of starring in this film so that you can choose your own path. With that

in mind, I have done the following reading to find out what you need to know about this situation in order to make the best decision about it. The cards I have dealt are as follows:

1. Advantages of making this film:
   Four of Wands reversed

2. Considerations to help you decide what to do:
   Nine of Cups reversed

3. Drawbacks to making this film:
   Queen of Wands

The first thing that I notice about this reading is that the cards for both of your choices—to do the movie or not to do it—are Wands cards. This indicates that at its root, the decision you face is not about things like money or your beliefs and ideals. Rather, it is about power, creativity, and risk. The questions you may want to explore to help you make this decision, then, are ones like, "Is your reluctance to do this movie a power or ego issue? Will working on this movie help you to express or exercise your creativity? Is doing it a reasonable risk?" Regarding that last question, it is important to remember that while it is prudent to avoid unreasonable risks, we never grow or gain anything without taking a chance.

As for the specific cards in this reading, let me begin with the first and third cards, which discuss the pros and cons of working on this film. Then we'll consider the middle card.

The reversed Four of Wands says that this film will help you break out of a box. Have your movies to date tended to cast you in a mold? Might it not be valuable for you to expand beyond that stereotype? This card suggests that working on this movie may help you do that. An entirely different take on this card comes from seeing the Four of Wands as a celebration, perhaps even a marriage. Being reversed, then, it might point toward the breakup of a marriage. This indicates that doing this movie may ultimately put you into a position where you can get a divorce that you want.

The Queen of Wands indicates that someone, perhaps your costar, will be a strong and willful woman with whom it may be difficult to work. More than that, this movie will be one in which the main star will not be you; it will be her. This interpretation is reinforced by the interesting correspondence between the name of the female lead (Scarlett), the fact that Wands are associated with fire (and thus with the color red), and a queen is female. Thus, this card says that a danger of doing this film lies in being overshadowed by the Red Woman—Scarlett O'Hara.

Now let me turn to the card that can help you decide how to handle this situation. First of all, the Nine of Cups is often called the *Wish Card,* but its reversal may indicate that your wishes are being delayed. So you might ask yourself if there is some wish of yours (such as a love interest) that you are impatient to fulfill. Perhaps that impatience is affecting your decision about making this film. If so, this card indicates that your wish will come true, but it will just take some time.

This card also says that at this time you may be overly smug and satisfied with your career. Like the man on this card with his nine cups lined up proudly on a table behind him, you may feel that you have it all now. What might be hidden behind the blue drape on the table? Is there more than what is apparent in your life so far? This card asks you to consider if doing this film might help you find some sort of hidden fulfillment, such as contentment within yourself or an improvement of your craft.

I hope these considerations are of assistance as you make your decision.

Best of luck to you,
KnightHawk

Comments on a Reading with the Decision Spread

It is ironic that Clark Gable did not want to play Rhett Butler in *Gone with the Wind,* since this turned out to be his most endearing and memorable role. Besides having professional concerns about the movie, Gable was having trouble with his personal life at the time, which certainly must have played a part in his considerations. As we know, he did end up making the film, and it worked out well for him—professionally and personally.

Gable was still married to his second wife, Rhea, at the time that this reading would have been done, although he had begun to have an affair with Carole Lombard. The studio executives wanted to avoid the scandal that this situation had the potential to create, so they pressured Gable to stop seeing Lombard. Instead, Gable ended up divorcing Rhea, and after *GWTW* was completed, he married Lombard. Considering the divorce aspect of the reversed Four of Wands, this reading implies that his success with this film may have helped him stand up to the studio, enabling him to do what he pleased with his love life.

One of the participants at the workshop that did this group reading for Clark Gable asked why I chose a Decision spread for this reading instead of a Problem/Advice spread (described at the end of this section). The answer is that choosing what type of spread to use involves a good deal of intuition nurtured by experience, but there are some rational guidelines that I find useful as well. In this case, I saw Gable's question as more of a decision for him to make than as a problem for him to solve, and so I used the Decision spread. This was, of course, a judgment call, and a Problem/Advice spread could have been used for there is usually more than one way to tackle any problem.

Another interesting note about this reading is the fact that it contained one of those curiously spine-tingling literalisms that sometimes arise during a Tarot reading.[10] In light of the fact that *Gone with the Wind* received nine Oscars (if we include the honorary one it got for Use of Color for the Enhancement of Dramatic Mood), consider the image of the nine cups lined up like trophies in the Nine of Cups card. It is possible that in 1938 a Tarot reader with particularly prescient psychic abilities may have been able to glean from this image the fact that this film would win nine Oscars. However, I am making this observation here in this comments section rather than including it in the reading itself because such an impressive insight is beyond the typical Tarot reader. Thus, its inclusion in the reading would have been of little educational value, and instead may have seemed like cheating or grandstanding through the use of hindsight.

---

10. I define a literalism as an image on a card that bears a strikingly literal resemblance to something about the querent, his or her situation, or the question for the reading.

Specific Notes About Individual Positions in the Spread

POSITION ONE: ADVANTAGES OF MAKING THIS FILM

When the first card in this spread seems to be more dire than advantageous, it can be a challenge to interpret it. Every card has a full spectrum of meaning, though, so it is just a matter of finding the positive aspects of the card. In this section's reading, the Four of Wands could have been easy to interpret in this position had it not been reversed. Since it was, I had to dig a bit deeper to find the positive message that "this film will help you break out of a box," which was partly based on the fact that Fours are associated with structure, and structures that are too rigid sometimes can be stultifying. The relevance of this message can be seen in the following note about Gable's work in *Gone with the Wind*.

Soon after shooting began on the movie, the director, George Cukor, was fired. His replacement was Victor Fleming, with whom Gable got along very well. Due to their friendship, Fleming was able to induce the star to give a better performance than would otherwise have been the case. Perhaps the best example of this was in the scene where Rhett Butler's daughter dies. For that scene, Fleming was able to persuade Gable to do something he had never done on-screen before, which was to cry. As a result, that scene enriched the actor's public persona, and it endeared him to his fans more than ever.

POSITION TWO: CONSIDERATIONS TO HELP YOU DECIDE WHAT TO DO

While the first and third positions directly deal with the pros and cons of taking a specific course of action, the card in the middle position often addresses the issue at hand more indirectly or tangentially. The considerations it presents may be about the proposed alternatives, but they also can be about peripheral topics that do have a bearing upon the reading and that the querent needs to consider in making his decision.

In the reading for Clark Gable, card 2 noted general concerns about his career that he needed to think about before making this specific career decision. However, it also brought up a seemingly unrelated topic (unfulfilled wishes "such as a love interest") and asked him to consider how it might affect, or be affected by, this decision.

POSITION THREE: DRAWBACKS TO MAKING THIS FILM

The final card can present a challenge similar to that of the first one. If this card seems optimistic, fortunate, or promising, it can be hard to see how it might indicate a disadvantage. Again, with a bit of perseverance, the drawback it represents can be found. For example, at first glance, the cheerful Queen of Wands in the Clark Gable reading does not seem to be a problem. However, when this court card is viewed as another person, rather than as a personality trait of the querent's, its message is brought to light in the form of the willful Vivien Leigh playing the headstrong Scarlett O'Hara.

Other Notes About This Spread

As the reading for Clark Gable illustrates, the value of comparing cards 1 and 3 (Pros and Cons) can go beyond finding a contrast in their meanings. It is also valuable to try to see if there are any subtle similarities or differences in these cards that might make a general statement about the decision that the querent faces. For example, is there a predominant color common to both, or are they both court cards, or Aces, or major arcana cards? In the reading for Clark Gable, both of these cards were in the suit of Wands, which indicated that his decision was about power, creativity, and risk.

On occasion, cards 1 and 3 may present the querent with a clear choice if the pro argument is substantially more compelling than the con, or vice versa. Unfortunately, our decisions in life are rarely that clear cut or easy. The querent may be left with the task of carefully weighing approximately equal pros and cons, although the considerations raised by the second card can help. A reading with the Decision spread will leave the querent better informed and thus better able to make his decision.

Alternative Spreads

The spread used for the reading in this section is one of a vast number of three-card spreads. I have either created or come across dozens of such spreads, and I continue to do so. Fortunately, many three-card spreads share some common thematic structures, and this facilitates a useful system of categorization, which is described below.

TEMPORAL SPREADS

Temporal or time-oriented spreads are useful in general readings wherein querents do not articulate a specific problem or choice they need to deal with. The most common example of this type of spread is the Past, Present, Future spread. If we shift the time frame a bit, it yields another temporal spread with the following positions:

1. Present

2. Near or immediate future

3. More distant future

PROBLEM/ADVICE SPREADS

These spreads work well for questions about how to handle or solve a specific problem. There are two basic forms of this type of three-card spread, as noted below. The first one includes background information, such as where the querent is coming from or how the problem developed. The second one examines the probable outcome instead.

1. Background

2. Problem

3. Advice

Or:

1. Problem

2. Advice

3. Probable outcome

Of course, these two spreads can be combined to create the following four-card spread:

1. Background

2. Problem

3. Advice

4. Probable outcome

LEVELS OF BEING SPREADS

These spreads examine basic levels of the querent's being. They are useful for doing general readings, but they also can examine a specific problem by seeing how it affects, or is affected by, these different facets of the querent's life. Considering the querent's body, mind, and emotions leads to a spread like this:

1. How is your health or physical resources being affected by this situation?

2. What are your thoughts or beliefs about it?

3. What are your feelings about it?

Using a triad like thought, word, and deed can give us the following spread:

1. What do you or someone else think about this situation?

2. What is being communicated about it?

3. What is being done about it?

If we want to look at the three areas of a querent's life that probably are the most frequent subjects of Tarot readings, this spread might work well:

1. How is your love life being affected?

2. How is your career being affected?

3. How are your finances being affected?

YES OR NO SPREADS

There are two basic types of yes/no questions that querents often ask. The first is, "Will this event happen?" and the second is, "Should I take this action?" The first implies that the querent is powerless to affect his or her future, and the second implies that the querent wants us to be responsible for his or her decision. Neither of these are viable conditions, so I like to use the following spread that gives querents information to shape their own future or to make their own decisions instead.

1. Yes if . . .

2. No if . . .

3. Maybe if . . .

The first two cards may be considered signs. As an example, let's say a man wonders if he should ask his girlfriend to marry him. If these two cards are perhaps the Two of Cups and the Five of Pentacles, respectively, they might say, "Yes, you should ask your girlfriend to marry you if the two of you have a loving relationship. No, you shouldn't if your financial situation is bad right now."

Alternatively, these cards might be considered as providing advice. For example, if this reading were for this man's girlfriend to see if he is going to propose to her, the same two cards might tell her, "Yes, he will ask you to marry him if you become more emotionally involved with him. No, he won't if you cannot moderate your financial needs, which he may think seem bound to impoverish him."

The third card provides messages of a more general nature. If we consider the first two cards to be signs, this one may provide food for thought on the subject of the reading. Using the first of the above examples, if the third card is the Seven of Pentacles, it might say to this man, "Whether or not you should ask her to marry you depends on how carefully you have examined what you want out of a marriage to this woman."

On the other hand, if we see the first two cards as giving advice, then the third one may suggest an alternative course. In the second example, the Seven of Pentacles might tell the girlfriend, "He might ask you to marry him, but you should reconsider what you want from this relationship before it can become a viable possibility."

CHOICE SPREADS

When querents ask about making a choice between two options, they again may be trying to get us to take responsibility for their decision. In that case, the following spread can be empowering for querents in that it provides information that enables them to make their own informed decision.

1. Choice A

2. Deciding factor/alternative choice

3. Choice B

The first and third cards can be used in one of several different ways. They can indicate the probable outcome of these choices, the advantages of them, their disadvantages, or general considerations about them. The middle card can indicate something in the querent's life that can help him or her make this choice, or it can indicate either a completely different alternative the querent should consider or a compromise between the two choices. Thus, there are about a dozen variations on this one basic spread. For example, the following are a couple of specific Choice spreads:

1. Advantages of taking choice A

2. A deciding factor to help you choose between these two options

3. Advantages of taking choice B

And:

1. Probable outcome of taking choice A

2. A compromise between these two options

3. Probable outcome of taking choice B

Note that the Decision spread used for Clark Gable's reading is a variant of the Choice spread.

I have discovered and developed more three-card spreads than I have presented here. Many such spreads do not conveniently fit into these categories, but the above examples should provide a fairly comprehensive overview of this subject.[11] You can use them in your Tarot readings, or they can be a catalyst for you to create your own three-card spreads.

---

11. The categorization scheme presented here may seem somewhat arbitrary, but it is a useful place to start thinking about three-card spreads and to look for ideas for such spreads.

THE YIN-YANG SPREAD
A Two-Card Spread

Like their three-card cousins, two-card Tarot spreads may seem trifling at first glance, so some people discount them. There is, however, power in the simplicity of such spreads, and they should not be disregarded so lightly. Indeed, the considerations of duality that two-card spreads often afford can lead to surprisingly profound insights. They can focus on contrasting or complementary aspects of an issue, such as its pros and cons or its spiritual and material aspects. Thus, they can lead to a deeper understanding of an issue by pointing toward a more balanced view of it.

In order to understand two-card spreads better, let us first look at a classic expression of duality: the ancient Chinese principle of yin and yang. This is symbolized as follows:

This is probably the oldest expression of the inherent duality of the cosmos that we know of today. In brief, yin (the black half of the circle) symbolizes things like passivity, receptivity, that which is mysterious, and darkness, while yang (the white half) symbolizes things like activity, initiative, that which is known, and light. Yin and yang are not antagonistic entities, however. Instead, they are mutually dependent and complementary. For example, a decision to take a specific action also defines that which we have not chosen to do (and vice versa).

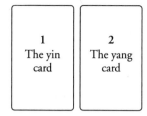

Figure 9. The Yin-Yang spread.

Based on this philosophy, I decided to create a two-card spread in which the first card represents the yin aspects of the reading, and the second, the yang. To create such a spread, I began by thinking about yin-yang pairs, and I came up with dualities such as past/future, pro/con, and light/dark. These seemed either too cliché or too unremarkable, so I went on to consider less-obvious pairs, such as contemplation/action, unforeseen/ expected, and surrender/defend. This new list led me to several pairs of positional meanings that I thought would work well in a two-card spread.

As I tried to narrow down my choice to just one such pair, however, I realized that most of them would work well in harmony with each other. This led me to the interesting idea of creating a layout that is intended to be interpreted successively through different spread definitions. Since this was to be a spread for two cards using the concept of duality, I decided to use two such pairs of questions. The result was the following spread.

The Spread

Begin by dealing two cards side by side as in Figure 9.

First, interpret these two cards based on the following pair of questions:

Card 1: What, in this situation, do you need to release?

Card 2: What should you hold on to?

Next, interpret them based on these two questions:

Card 1: What do you need to consider further about your situation or problem?

Card 2: What action might you take to resolve it?

Finally, for additional insights, compare the two card 1 answers, and then do the same for the two card 2 answers. This will shed light on the general yin and yang aspects of the querent's situation.

A KnightHawk Reading with the Yin-Yang Spread

Dear KnightHawk,

My sister, the Lady Madeline, is no more. Since she must be preserved for a fortnight until a place for her body is ready in our family burial ground, a friend has helped me entomb her temporarily in a vault beneath our home.

My initial grief, however, is now turning to horror. You see, I have an affliction by which I suffer a morbid acuteness of the senses, and I have begun to hear strange sounds. I fear that they are the sounds of my sister struggling to escape her coffin.

What in God's name is happening? Have we put her living in the tomb? What am I to do?

Respectfully yours,
Roderick Usher

*   *   *

Dear Mr. Usher,

Thank you for asking me to read for this very unique question. I have asked the cards to provide insights into your situation to help you understand how to deal with it effectively. To that end, I have dealt the following cards:

1. Strength reversed

2. Seven of Swords reversed

First we shall see what these cards have to say about what you may need to let go of and what you would do well to hold on to. In addition, these cards will suggest what you need to understand regarding your situation and what you might do about it. Before delving into the details of this reading, though, let me make a couple of general comments about these cards.

First, since both cards are reversed, I see that there is much more here than meets the eye. Indeed, the mysterious and the unknown predominate in your life right

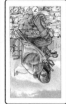

now. Next, my initial consideration of these two cards is that the reversed Strength card indicates your sense of helplessness, and the reversed Seven of Swords signifies self-deception.

Specifically, then, the advice of the reversed Strength card is to let go of your sense of helplessness. Realize your own strength and access it in order to conquer your fears. The reversed Seven of Swords, on the other hand, advises you to hold on to that which seems to be self-delusion. It urges you to pay heed to your superstitions, for something that seems irrational to you may turn out to be quite reasonable after all.

Returning to the reversed Strength card, I also see a couple of things that you need to consider about what is going on around you. First, the death of your sister has robbed you of your strength. My second observation comes from digging deeper into the message of this card in an attempt to understand how her death could have done so. What I see is that you had given away your strength to her, and so when you entombed her, you sealed up your strength as well. Fortunately, this suggests that what once was yours to give away might be yours to reclaim again, which leads us again to the Seven of Swords.

The action suggested by the reversed Seven of Swords may be understood by seeing this card as saying, "Uncover the deception." In other words, reveal what is hidden. Applying this advice to your specific situation, I see that this card recommends that you return to your sister's tomb and open her coffin. If she was entombed alive, this will save her. If not, at least your concerns may be laid to rest.

In summary, the reversed Strength card urges you to look inside yourself in order to find and reclaim the strength you have denied and given away. The reversed Seven of Swords advises you to heed what seems to be a superstitious notion and investigate your sister's tomb. Together, these cards say that the strength you can find inside yourself will enable you to take this action, which can resolve the situation you are in.

Thank you for letting me read for you, Mr. Usher. I hope this reading is of assistance to you.

Best of luck to you,
KnightHawk

Comments on a Reading with the Yin-Yang Spread

For the sake of those who have not read Edgar Allan Poe's "The Fall of the House of Usher," the following is a brief synopsis of the story.

Roderick Usher, a man debilitated by a strange malady, lives with his twin sister, the Lady Madeline. She, too, is sick, but hers is a very different affliction, and she soon dies (we presume). Her brother entombs her in a vault beneath the house since, for rather bizarre reasons, she cannot be buried for a fortnight. Within days Usher begins to hear strange sounds, until one stormy night the Lady Madeline crashes into his room and collapses upon him. They both fall dead, and soon their house itself cracks, crumbles, and collapses into a stagnant lake adjacent to it.

This tale is an early, and quintessential, gothic horror story. Over the years, it has been subject to a variety of disparate interpretations, and so I was eager to examine it through the magnifying lens of a Tarot reading in order to deepen my own understanding of it. The conclusion I came to as a result of this reading was that the Lady Madeline represents Roderick Usher's anima, of which he tries to rid himself.[12] This denial of a part of himself saps his vitality and culminates in his demise. As we can see, this story, which deals with the life and death of a brother and a sister (one weak and one strong), is rich in dualistic themes, as were both the spread I used and the reading that resulted from it.

First of all, when considered on a purely visual level, the two cards in this reading form a striking yin-yang pair. The Strength card's bright yellow hues are yang to the yin of the Seven of Sword's somber blue-gray tones. However, since the yang-colored Strength card is in the yin position, while the yang card (Seven of Swords) has yin coloring, these cards form a sort of reversed yin-yang pair. This observation added weight to the interpretation of mystery and delusion that I inferred from the fact that both cards are in a reversed aspect.

---

12. A man's anima is his inner (and often repressed) feminine nature, just as a woman's animus is her inner masculine nature. This concept of the anima turns out to be one of several dualistic elements of this tale.

I also noticed that these two cards seemed to depict the two major characters of this tale. The Strength card could easily be seen as Lady Madeline, who had the strength to escape her tomb (or to return from death, depending on how one interprets this tale). Similarly, the Seven of Swords may be seen as indicating Roderick Usher, from whom something was taken (his strength) that he desperately needed to reclaim. Also, one school of thought about this story postulates that Usher knew that his sister was not dead when he nailed her in her coffin, which would be the ultimate Seven of Swords act of treachery, betrayal, and deceit.

As I proceeded to interpret these cards within the context of their positional meanings, I encountered a problem. At first I was at a loss as to how to see the reversed Seven of Swords as an indication of something to hold on to. Then I realized that Usher's seemingly superstitious belief about the nature of the sounds he was hearing could be seen as self-delusion, which led to another expression of dualism in the ironic statement, ". . . something that seems irrational to you may turn out to be quite reasonable after all."

Finally, when I compared card 1's answers to its first question ("What, in this situation, do you need to release?") with its answers to its second question ("What do you need to understand about your situation or problem?"), I found a consistency of theme. There was a similar consistency of theme for card 2. The Strength card first advised Usher to let go of his helplessness, and then it explained the cause of that helplessness. The Seven of Swords suggested that he pay attention to a seeming self-delusion, and then advised him to investigate it. These considerations led to the summary at the end of this reading.

Although this sort of thematic consistency is typical, it may not always be the case. When a card's answer to its first question seems in contrast to its answer to its second question, there may be distinct alternatives that the querent needs to explore. On the other hand, perhaps an effort to resolve this apparent discrepancy can lead to a better understanding of what that card is trying to say.

Alternative Spreads

Instead of using each of the cards in the Yin-Yang spread twice, we could use the two pairs of questions given in the Yin-Yang spread to create a four-card spread. In that case, we could deal two cards that will use the first pair of questions, and under them two more for the second pair of questions, as follows:

Card 1: What, in this situation, do you need to release?

Card 2: What should you hold on to?

Card 3: What do you need to understand about your situation or problem?

Card 4: What action might you take to resolve it?

On the other hand, consideration of the concepts outlined at the beginning of this section may suggest other yin-yang combinations, such as advantages and disadvantages, destiny and freedom of choice, or your perspective and someone else's point of view. We can use any such yin-yang pairs to create different questions for the Yin-Yang spread. For example, consider the following:

Pair one:

Card 1: What spiritual lessons can you learn from your situation?

Card 2: What, on a material or physical plane, should you do about your situation?

Pair two:

Card 1: What may be an unexpected consequence of this situation?

Card 2: How do you expect it to turn out?

THE MAGICAL TRIANGLE SPREAD
A Four-Card Spread

At the 1999 Los Angeles Tarot Symposium, I attended a workshop called "Magical Triangles: A Model of Interaction." In that workshop, the presenter, Alexandra Genetti, noted that almost every action can be diagrammed as a triangle with a point in the center, like this:

Here, the first corner of the triangle corresponds to the actor; the second, to the object of the action; the third, to the action itself; and the center point corresponds to the result of the action. Alternatively, we can consider the first and second positions as two entities (perhaps people) that act upon or are in opposition to each other. In this case the third position can represent their interaction, with the center point representing the result of their interaction.

That workshop inspired me to consider what spreads might be created based upon this diagram using the concepts associated with magical triangles.[13] I developed several such

---

13. Alexandra Genetti, creator of several Tarot decks, presents an extensive discussion about magical triangles in the book that accompanies her *Wheel of Change Tarot*.

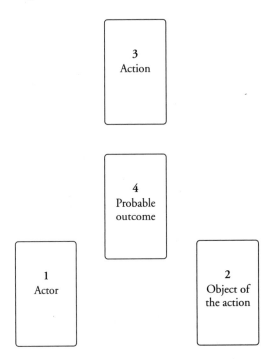

Figure 10. The Magical Triangle spread.

spreads, one of which is used in this section's reading, while others are presented at the end of this section under the heading "Alternative Spreads."

The Magical Triangle spread used in this section is best suited for readings where the querent is curious about the implications and results of a proposed course of action. However, if we make the querent the object of the action instead of the actor, it can explore how someone else's actions may affect him or her.

The Spread

Begin by dealing four cards as indicated in Figure 10.

Interpret these cards using the following positional meanings:

1. **The actor.** This card generally refers to the querent, but it may be someone in the querent's life.

2. **The object of the proposed action.** The object of the action may be a person or a thing. For example, it could be a person the querent wants to marry or a vacation

he or she plans to take. Alternatively, if the actor is someone other than the querent, then the object probably will be the querent.

3. **The action.** This card discusses what the querent needs to know about a proposed or anticipated course of action.

4. **The probable outcome.** This card describes the probable result of this action. This forecast is based on where the querent is right now in his or her life and the direction in which he or she is headed, as well as on considerations about the object of the proposed action.

A KnightHawk Reading with the Magical Triangle Spread

Dear KnightHawk,

My father has captured the leader of an expedition of white men—a man named John Smith—and plans to execute him. I think Father is making a mistake, however. These white men can be powerful allies . . . or dangerous foes. We would do well to have their friendship, so I plan to save John Smith's life. What can you tell me about this course of action? What will happen if I attempt this rescue?

With fondest regards,
Pocahontas

* * *

Dear Pocahontas,

Thank you for this interesting question. I have done a reading for you to see what you need to know about your plan to save John Smith. This reading examines various aspects of your proposed course of action by using a spread that addresses your question from several different points of view.

1. **You.** What are your motivations, and how well are you prepared to take this action?
   Nine of Swords

2. **John Smith's life.** What do you need to know about him, and about saving his life?
   Hierophant reversed

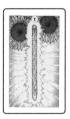

3. **The action.** Is your rescue plan viable and well conceived?
Ace of Wands reversed

4. **Probable outcome.** What is the probable result of this course of action?
The Star reversed

First of all, a general comment about this reading is that each card in it seems to express a certain degree of difficulty for your proposed action. Three out of the four cards are reversed (which can indicate problems or blockages), and the one that is not reversed is a somewhat problematic card anyway. Thus, this spread advises a great deal of care and caution as you consider this course of action, for there may be unknown factors underlying the situation you face, and your actions may have unforeseen or undesirable consequences.

Turning now to the specific cards here, the Nine of Swords indicates things like worry, guilt, and shame. From your question, I see that you are worried about the fate of your people, and to some extent, that worry is part of your motivation for taking this action. Additionally, however, I see that you also are worried about the results of this action. How will it affect the peace and tranquility of your life? Will it harm your relationship with your father and with your people in general? These worries feed your sense of guilt about following your planned course of action. Consequently, I see both motivations and obstacles in this card. It suggests that you should examine your motivations to see if they are valid, and that you need to face your fears to see if you are ready for this course of action and where it may lead you.

The next card, the reversed Hierophant, represents John Smith, and it makes the obvious comment that he is an outsider. More than that, however, it also suggests that as such, he may initiate the downfall of your society's social and spiritual order. Similarly, it implies that he represents your own rejection of the codes and mores that you have been taught. Considered specifically as a comment on Smith's character, this card warns that he can be dogmatic, self-righteous, and hypocritical, which is an analysis of him that may affect your decision about the course of action you are considering.

Next, the reversed Ace of Wands says that this action is a daunting challenge that will require you to access deep reserves of energy, passion, and determination. It also indicates that this situation is an opportunity for growth and change, but although you are ready for change, this may not be the right opportunity. Thus, this card counsels you to seriously reconsider initiating this action.

Finally, the reversed Star card indicates betrayed hope, disillusionment, and unrealistic or unattainable goals. Thus, this card says that the benefits you hope to gain through this action are unlikely or will be blocked and difficult to attain. However, this card does hold out the prospect of eventually finding peace, but that potential outcome will take quite a bit of time, and there will be some storms to get through before that time of tranquility can be reached. Even then, that peace may be transitory.

In conclusion, this reading advises extreme caution, for this may be an ill-advised course of action. Saving John Smith's life in anticipation of befriending his people probably will not satisfy your hope for a brighter future for your people. Indeed, it seems that Smith (and that which he represents) ultimately poses a danger to your people's way of life.

Thank you for requesting this reading, Pocahontas. I hope it helps you.

Best of luck to you!
KnightHawk

Comments on a Reading with the Magical Triangle Spread

According to the legend of Pocahontas's life, the Native American maiden saved Captain John Smith's life by using her own body as a shield when he was about to be clubbed to death. The veracity of this account, however, is highly suspect. Some scholars say that what Smith mistook for an execution was in reality a sort of adoption ritual in which Pocahontas undertook responsibility for his life. Others maintain that the entire account, which was not reported by Smith until many years later, was pure fiction that he fabricated based on popular stories and myths of the Native Americans.

With such a variety of interpretations of Smith's account, we probably will never know if Pocahontas really did save his life. This left me in a bit of a quandary as I prepared to do the reading for this section. How should I have Pocahontas pose her question? Which version of what happened between her and John Smith should I use?

After some deliberation, I decided to use the popular legend, whether or not it has a factual basis, since it is the story that most people know. If this legend is pure fiction, so be it. After all, many of the other "Ask KnightHawk" readings that I have done have been for fictional circumstances, so why not this one too?

With that decision made, I next had to pose Pocahontas's question for her, and to do so, I had to think about why she wanted to save Smith's life. Had she fallen in love with him, or was her plan a pragmatic one based on considerations of power and security? Or was her reasoning along entirely different lines altogether? To settle this issue, I did a quick one-card reading and got the Emperor. Based on that, it was clear that her question was not about love. The Emperor indicated to me that Pocahontas's decision was based on things like power, control, and protecting her people, and the phrasing of her question evolved from there.

The preceding discussion of the circumstances that set the stage for this section's reading provides a context in which the reading can be viewed and understood. In addition, though, the following comments about the consequences of Pocahontas's action are also helpful in comprehending it.

Pocahontas's friendship with the English settlers at Jamestown did eventually lead to peace between the Native Americans and the English, which lasted for eight years following her marriage to Virginia colonist John Rolf in 1614. However, this "peace of Pocahontas" did not begin until about six years after she met Captain John Smith, and in 1622 (five years after Pocahontas's death), hostilities broke out again. Over the course of the next few decades her people were massacred and their culture was all but obliterated.

In the process of doing Pocahontas's reading, I gained a better perspective of the long-term impact of this young woman's interaction with the English. When we Americans of European descent think about Pocahontas at all, we generally say something like, "Wasn't that nice of Pocahontas to save John Smith's life!" True, it may have been generous and altruistic, but Pocahontas's people may have been much better off if they had tried to expel the English before they were able to establish a strong foothold at Jamestown, Virginia. In fact, saving John Smith's life and befriending the English may have marked the beginning of the end for Pocahontas's people.[14] It is a sad irony that Pocahontas's act of compassion may have had the dire consequence of destroying her people and their culture. Today we revere Pocahontas as a heroine, but after doing this reading, I wondered how her own people viewed her.

On the other hand, our common perception is that Pocahontas's rescue of John Smith was performed with a youthful fervor that was naïve and rash. A Tarot reading often yields insights for the reader as well as for the querent, and in this case, the Nine of Swords told me that that Pocahontas's rescue of Smith was not impulsive. In supporting Smith and the English in general, she may have betrayed her own people to some extent, but I saw in this reading that she did not do this without suffering doubt and worry beforehand, and some anguish and regret afterward.

Specific Notes About Individual Positions in the Spread

The four positions in the Magical Triangle spread are defined in rather general terms and can work well that way when the reader is not aware of the background for the reading. Usually, however, it is a good idea to customize a spread's positional definitions to fit the particular circumstances of each reading whenever possible. So if we do have some knowledge of the background of the reading, then the positions in this spread may be restated to meet the specific needs of the reading. This was done for Pocahontas's reading, as indicated in the customized positional definitions that follow.

---

14. Whether or not the legend of Pocahontas saving Smith's life is true, Pocahontas did befriend the English, and in general her people were friendly and helpful to the struggling Jamestown settlers through their first difficult years. Without Smith's leadership, and without the benign relationship between the English and Pocahontas's people that the young Native American princess helped establish, Jamestown may have failed in its infancy.

POSITION ONE: YOU. WHAT ARE YOUR MOTIVATIONS, AND HOW WELL ARE YOU PRE-PARED TO TAKE THIS ACTION?

The card in the first position discusses what the querent needs to know about herself relative to her proposed action. For example, is she ready and able to take this action, or is she ill prepared for it? What does she think of this action? How does she feel about it? What are her hopes or fears about taking this action? Questions such as these can be used to customize this position in the spread.

The card in this position also can point out the querent's strengths and weaknesses that are relevant to the proposed action, and it can comment on her motivations for taking this action and on the internal obstacles she faces in doing so.

POSITION TWO: JOHN SMITH'S LIFE. WHAT DO YOU NEED TO KNOW ABOUT HIM, AND ABOUT SAVING HIS LIFE?

This card addresses the pertinent issues concerning the object of the proposed action. If the object is a person, which it usually is, it may reveal if he is amenable to the proposed action or resistant to it. It may note how he stimulates or incites that action, or how he may be affected by it. However, considerations about this person should be limited to their relevance to that action. It is unethical to use a reading with this spread as an excuse for a fishing expedition to dredge up secrets about someone else.

Alternatively, if the object of the action is not a person, the considerations that may arise include things like how it will be affected by the action or how it might affect the execution of the action. For example, this card may indicate risks or obstacles that the object of the action poses in and of itself.

POSITION THREE: THE ACTION. IS YOUR RESCUE PLAN VIABLE AND WELL CONCEIVED?

The third card usually discusses the challenges of the querent's action. For example, it may point out any pitfalls or roadblocks that she should watch out for. Similarly, it may forecast the ease or difficulty with which she will be able to undertake this action.

Also, some cards may encourage the querent to undertake this course of action, while others may seem discouraging instead. More frustrating (to the querent, at least) are those that present a rather balanced or neutral message wherein the pros and cons of taking action are nearly equal. In any case, remember that it is up to the querent to evaluate everything in the reading, including the message of this card, in order to come to her own decision.

Position Four: Probable Outcome. What Is the Probable Result of This Course of Action?

Since the probable outcome depends greatly on considerations about the querent, the proposed action, and the object of that action, the meaning of this final card is strongly affected by the interpretations of the preceding three cards. For example, in the reading for Pocahontas, I interpreted the reversed Star card more darkly than I may have otherwise because of the dire tone set by the preceding three cards. Of course, the probable outcome that this card forecasts may be altered by the querent's future decisions and actions now that she has been forewarned.

Other Notes About This Spread

In the preceding discussions, I generally have referred to card 3 as being about the querent's proposed action, which assumes that this spread is designed to help the querent decide whether or not to take an action. However, this spread also can be used to help the querent examine and comprehend a proposed, feared, or desired action that someone else may (or may not) take. In that case, that other person will be the actor (card 1), and the querent probably will be the object of the action (card 2).

Alternative Spreads

Based on the concepts concerning magical triangles that were described at the beginning of this section, there are other spreads that can use the same basic four-card layout but with different positional meanings. The following are several suggestions, but feel free to play with these ideas in order to design your own spreads.

    A. The Relationship Magical Triangle spread

        1. The querent

        2. A friend, lover, or family member

        3. Their relationship

        4. Where their relationship is headed

    B. The Conflict Magical Triangle spread

        1. The querent

        2. Someone with whom the querent is in conflict

THE SORROW'S ALCHEMY SPREAD
A Four-Card Spread

Years ago, I came across the following quote, which was attributed to Pearl S. Buck: "Sorrow, fully accepted, brings its own gifts, for there is an alchemy in sorrow. It can be transmuted into wisdom, which if it does not bring joy, can yet bring happiness." This quote grabbed my attention, for it reflects what I believe to be one of the best uses of a Tarot reading: to examine a querent's problems in order to work with him or her to find transformative solutions to those problems. Consequently, I was moved to create a spread based on this quote, which resulted in this section's Sorrow's Alchemy spread.

This sort of inspiration is a powerful place to begin creating a spread, and it can lead to one that facilitates very insightful readings. In fact, any statement of universal truths—from a quote to a novel, from a simple haiku to an epic poem, or from a folktale to a Homeric myth—may inspire a new spread, and my design of the Sorrow's Alchemy spread illustrates this fact.

The first step in this process was to distill the basic elements of the above quote into specific card positions. Of course, the identification of the most pertinent aspects of a quote is a highly personal choice. In this case, I found four essential elements: sorrow, transformation, wisdom, and happiness. From these, I derived the questions that define the four card positions in this section's spread.

Next, I drew up a pattern in which to lay down these four cards, which is another intuitive process. I try to consider what pattern the meanings of the card positions suggest. For this spread, I began by placing three of the positions in a line, based on this quote's concept that *sorrow transformed* can lead to *happiness.* I then put *wisdom,* an attribute I associate with our higher self, above the other positions. Specifically, I placed it above transformation because it is a result of that function.

As for the use of this spread, I find that it is an excellent tool for helping people deal with loss, including (but not limited to) the death of a loved one. Also, this spread is unusual in that it is well suited for doing readings to help us deal with our own sorrow. Self-readings generally are hard to do because the insistent voice of our ego tends to over-power our intuition, and this is especially true when the soft voice of our intuition is pre-senting painful truths or suggesting a difficult course of action. However, this spread, being less about decisions and evaluations than most other spreads, provides fewer oppor-tunities for ego intrusion. Instead, being tailored more for personal transformation than for problem solving or prediction, it tends to activate the intuitive functions of contem-plation and introspection during self-readings.

As suggested above, we can create a spread using anything that inspires us, touches our heart, or suggests a new way of seeing the world. As we pay closer and closer attention to everything around us, we inevitably will begin to find inspiration for spreads everywhere we look; the universe is filled with sources of universal truths. We can make such discov-eries in the most unlikely or unexpected places too: an intense experience, a disturbing dream, a beautiful painting, a haunting melody, an evocative poem, or a profound quote. Any of these may suggest a new spread; we just have to be open and receptive to such inspiration.

The Spread
Begin by dealing four cards as indicated in Figure 11.

Interpret these cards using the following questions:

1. What sorrow are you experiencing and what do you need to understand about it?

2. How might you transmute this sorrow and thus transform your life?

3. What wisdom can you gain in the process?

4. What happiness awaits you beyond this experience?

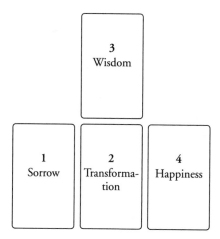

Figure 11. The Sorrow's Alchemy spread.

A KnightHawk Reading with the Sorrow's Alchemy Spread

Dear KnightHawk,

When I was a young girl, I met a boy named Peter Pan and we shared many wonderful adventures together in a place called the Neverland. He was a lovely boy, carefree and innocent, and every day with him was fun and exciting. But, alas, I had to return home eventually.

Twice Peter has returned to take me back with him to do his spring cleaning. But he was always a forgetful boy, living only in the present moment, and it has been several years now since his last visit. I dearly miss him and the joy he brought me, and as I grow up, I see the gap between us yawn ever wider. I fear that now we shall be forever parted, and that makes me very sad.

What can I do? How can I make this sadness go away?

Love,
Wendy Darling

*   *   *

Dear Wendy,

Thank you for asking me to help you deal with this sadness. I have asked the cards to suggest how you might overcome the sorrow you face and the cards I dealt are these:

1. What do you need to understand about your sadness?
   The Devil reversed

2. How might you transmute this sorrow and thus transform your life?
   Four of Wands

3. What wisdom can you gain in the process?
   Six of Cups reversed

4. What happiness awaits you beyond this sorrow?
   Two of Swords reversed

The Devil card illustrates the philosophical point that it is our attachment to the things we have lost that causes us pain, not the loss itself. Being reversed, then, this card recommends that you release your attachment to Peter and to your adventures with him so that you can move on with your life. The specific image on this version of the Devil card is instructive in its depiction of two people trying to pull a treasure chest in two different directions. This says that you and Peter have your own paths to walk, paths that will lead the two of you in very different directions. Doing things with Peter now would only stop you from continuing along your life's true path, and it would pull him away from his own destiny as well. Take what solace you can in knowing that you both are progressing along your proper course.

Although the Devil card urges you to release your attachment to Peter, this does not mean you have to forget him. Instead, the next card, the Four of Wands, advises you to celebrate what you had with him, perhaps even throw a party in his memory. Indeed, such a party could be a rite of passage leading you into maturity. This may appear to contradict the advice of the first card, but really it does not. Attachment to the past and dwelling on the pain of a loss will keep you from healing, but the celebration advised by this card will help you release that attachment and move on with your life. It can leave you with happy memories instead of wistful longings, and it also can help you learn how to deal with loss in the future.

The Six of Cups can depict innocence and childhood memories, but being reversed, it says that the wisdom you can gain is the realization that now is the time for you to lay aside your childhood games and fantasies as you prepare to grow into adulthood. This does not mean you must reject the unconditional sharing and caring at which children are so adept, but rather that you need to understand that as you grow up, you must leave behind the simple innocence of your childhood.

The next card, the reversed Two of Swords, sees a difficult decision ahead for you. On the one hand, you do not want to grow up and leave Peter behind, but on the other hand, you must grow up and become an adult. Perhaps you are trying to find a compromise between these two forces, but since this card is reversed, it says that this is neither possible nor viable. In fact, this stalemate between those two factors in your life is what is causing you such pain, since you do not see how to reconcile them. If you take the advice of the prior cards in this reading, you will be able to see your way to make the right decision and break through this impasse. Then you will be able to release your pain and find happiness in your life—the joys of your adulthood.

In this reading, I see the pivotal card as being the one in the center: the Four of Wands. By focusing on it and viewing it as the central feature of a larger tableau, I see the following summarization of this reading: a celebration of your adventures with Peter can be a rite of passage for you that can help you let go of your attachment to your friendship with him and then grow beyond your childhood as you make the difficult decision to become an adult.

Thank you, Wendy, for requesting this reading. I hope it may be of some help to you.

Best of luck,
KnightHawk

Comments on a Reading with the Sorrow's Alchemy Spread

The moment I first saw Mary Martin dressed as Peter Pan fly through the nursery window of the Darling house, I fell in love with this delightful story. Although the title of the play is *Peter Pan,* the book was originally published as *Peter and Wendy,* which indicates that this story is about both children: the boy who would not grow up and the girl who had to.

Peter lived eternally in the here and now, forgetting about the past and not concerning himself with the future, so it seemed irrelevant, or even irreverent, to do a Tarot reading for him. Wendy, however, was another matter. She was no more immune to regrets and worry than the rest of us, and since she believed in magic, I think she would have loved getting a Tarot reading.

Although Wendy did return to the Neverland a couple of times to help Peter with his spring cleaning, there came a time when he stopped coming for her. So I imagined that it would have been after losing touch with Peter but before deciding to grow up and put the needs and desires of her childhood behind her that Wendy would have asked for this reading.

In almost every Tarot reading some cards are easy to interpret and others are not. This reading presented examples of both extremes. The first two cards turned out to be surprisingly appropriate for dealing with any loss with their advice to Wendy to celebrate what she had but also to release her attachments in order to move on. The third card, the Six of Cups, was also perfect for this particular reading since it deals with childhood, innocence, and sharing love.

It was the final card, however, that presented a challenge. What kind of happiness could the reversed Two of Swords foresee? Prior to laying out the cards I wondered if something would come up in this last position that would depict a joyful anticipation of Peter's eventual return (which happened many years later when Wendy had a little girl of her own), but I did not see that sort of message in the reversed Two of Swords. However, a deeper consideration of this card led me to its message for this reading, which was that Wendy needed to make the difficult decision to release the past and move forward in order to find happiness in her future.

In addition, this reading held a valuable message for me in addition to its message for Wendy. On the surface, *Peter Pan* seems to be a fantasy about the timeless wonders of youth, such as children's imagination and lust for adventure. However, the reversed Six of Cups said that this story is also about the inevitable bittersweet need to let go of our childhood. To this the reversed Two of Swords added the message that it can be hard to turn away from the magical allure of childhood and make the difficult decision to assume the responsibilities of adulthood. A deeper insight from this reading, though, was that this tale is about the delicate balance of letting go of the innocence and wonder of youth while still retaining a bit of its magic deep inside our hearts.

Specific Notes About Individual Positions in the Spread

POSITION ONE: WHAT DO YOU NEED TO UNDERSTAND ABOUT YOUR SADNESS?

This card may reveal unsuspected facets or aspects of the querent's sorrow of which she was previously unaware. More often, though, its comments delve deeper into the sorrow she already knows exists, providing her with a better understanding of it and recommending ways of dealing with it. In the situation for this reading, it was obvious that Wendy missed Peter Pan and their adventures together. The card in this position went beneath the surface of that sorrow, however, to provide the understanding that "it is our attachment to the things we have lost that causes us pain, not the loss itself."

In addition, since every card can offer advice based on its insights, it is appropriate to search for recommendations here even though it is the next position that is specifically intended to advocate a course of action. The difference is that the second card suggests ways of transforming sorrow into something positive, while the first card's advice tends more toward ways to cope with sorrow. This aspect of card 1 is especially valuable when there is any comfort to be found, such as this reading's consoling thought that Wendy and Peter were each traveling their own proper course.

POSITION TWO: HOW MIGHT YOU TRANSMUTE THIS SORROW AND THUS TRANSFORM YOUR LIFE?

The guidance that the card in this position provides is more specific than the general advice we may have found in the previous card. When seeking the counsel of this second card, try to see what it recommends that the querent do in order to transform her sorrow into something positive and to transform herself into a better person. For example, in this reading Wendy was advised that a celebration could change her wistful longings into happy memories. It also told her how to use this sad experience to help her grow up and move on to a new phase of her life.

POSITION THREE: WHAT WISDOM CAN YOU GAIN IN THE PROCESS?

Whenever we face adversity, we have an opportunity to learn and grow, and the more severe the misfortune, the greater the learning opportunity. Unfortunately, we rarely view our problems that way. Sorrow concentrates our attention on the painful aspects of our experiences, but if we can look at our trials and tribulations and see the lessons in them instead of just the sorrow, we can find wisdom and even some measure of comfort. This component of the transformative power of sorrow's alchemy is what the third card in this spread reveals.

The focus of this card differs from that of the previous one in that it is concerned with the querent's perspective and perceptions, whereas the previous card's advice is usually more action oriented. Changing her perspective, however, tends to be harder for a querent than taking action, so initially she may resist the wisdom presented by this card. In doing a reading with this spread, then, it is important for us to remember that we can guide the querent to the insights expressed by this card, but we cannot make her believe them. Hopefully, that will come with time.

In this section's reading for Wendy, the wisdom offered by the reversed Six of Cups was that the time had come for her to leave her childhood behind and to embark on the long road toward adulthood. This was important advice for a character in a story about a boy who refused to grow up and a girl who loved to visit him in his world of eternal youth.

POSITION FOUR: WHAT HAPPINESS AWAITS YOU BEYOND THIS SORROW?
The first three cards in this spread sometimes lead the querent through a dark and painful journey. First we examined her sorrow, and then we made recommendations that might not be easy for her to take. Since it is important that a reading give a querent whatever hope is available, the card in this last position is valuable in that it reveals a light at the end of the tunnel. Indeed, this is one of the things I like about this spread—that it ends on an upbeat note.

Unfortunately, sometimes finding a message of happiness in this last position can be difficult, depending on the card that comes up. For example, some people might find it hard to see a hopeful message in the Ten of Swords or the Tower card. However, the Ten of Swords, for instance, might say that things have gotten as bad as they are going to get and now (based on what seems to be a sunrise in the background on that card) they will start to improve. Or the Tower may indicate that although a crisis will force the querent out of familiar circumstances, her situation was constricting or stifling, so this release will give her the freedom to grow and explore her new opportunities.

In this section's reading, I faced this sort of difficulty with the reversed Two of Swords card. While this is not one of the most ominous cards in the deck, it is not a particularly cheerful one either. I had a hard time seeing what happiness it presented Wendy until I considered that the Two of Swords can represent a stalemate or avoiding a decision. Reversed, then, it seemed to indicate that Wendy would be able to make an appropriate decision enabling her to move on with her life successfully.

Other Notes About This Spread

In the Sorrow's Alchemy spread, the second position is usually the lynchpin of the reading. First of all, it provides advice for overcoming the problems brought up in the first card. More than that, though, it is the bridge that then leads to the next two cards, since it indicates the transformation that brings about the wisdom of the third card and that produces the happiness of the final card. Thus, those two cards should be examined in its light.

In this section's reading, the Four of Wands did indeed play an important part in the interpretation of the two subsequent cards: the Six of Cups and the Two of Swords. The Four of Wands often is seen as a depiction of marriage, but sometimes I see a more general interpretation in it. It can indicate celebrating the completion of a phase of life, such as a bar mitzvah or a high school graduation, or it can depict a rite of passage, as was noted in this reading. It was this last interpretation that led me to see that both the wisdom of the reversed Six of Cups and the happiness of the reversed Two of Swords concerned Wendy leaving her childhood behind and moving on with her life. Also, the Four of Wands suggested that the alchemy of her sorrow could be actualized by a celebration of her adventures with Peter, and that celebration could be the rite of passage that she needed in order to find happiness in moving on with her life.

Alternative Spreads

Let us consider again the quote that inspired the Sorrow's Alchemy spread: "**Sorrow,** fully accepted, brings its own gifts, for there is an alchemy in sorrow. It can be **transmuted** into **wisdom,** which if it does not bring joy, can yet bring **happiness.**" I have emphasized in bold letters the words that indicate the elements used as the basis of this spread. This is not the only way of dividing this quote into components, however. If we emphasize its aspects differently, we can derive a somewhat different spread. For example, we might focus on the following words: *sorrow, accepted, gifts, wisdom,* and *happiness.*

In that case, we might arrive at a spread with the following positional meanings:

1. What should you know about your sorrow?

2. How can you accept it?

3. What gifts are hidden in it?

4. What wisdom can you learn from it?

5. How can you transform your sorrow into happiness?

How, then, might we arrange these positions in a spread? In this case, I see acceptance (card 2) as the pivotal issue, so I would put that card in the middle. I consider wisdom (card 4) to be a blessing or a higher function, so I would place the fourth card above the second, and since acceptance leads to happiness (card 5), the fifth card should go after the second. Finally, the idea of something being hidden (the gifts of card 3) may be represented by placing that card on a lower level of the spread, so it should go under the acceptance card.

In addition to these considerations, the overall pattern that resulted from them complements the concept underlying this new spread. The layout of the cards looks like a cross, which is a symbol that implies the attainment of wisdom and the transcendence of material problems through surrender to a higher power. This alternative Sorrow's Alchemy spread is illustrated in Figure 12.

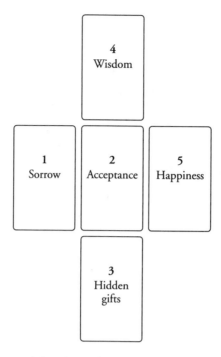

Figure 12. The Alternative Sorrow's Alchemy spread.

Finally, if you want to create your own spread based on a quote that inspires you, think of one or use one of the quotes listed below if you prefer, and use the technique described in this section. Creating such a spread will give you something to work with that is satisfying and meaningful since you will have invested something of yourself in it.

The following are several quotes that may inspire a Tarot spread:

1. "I try to avoid looking forward or backward, and try to keep looking upward." — Charlotte Brontë

2. "Destiny is not a matter of chance, it is a matter of choice; it is not a thing to be waited for, it is a thing to be achieved." —William Jennings Bryan

3. "... if one advances confidently in the direction of his dreams, and endeavors to live the life he has imagined, he will meet with a success unexpected in common hours." —Henry David Thoreau

4. "One doesn't discover new lands without consenting to lose sight of the shore for a very long time." —Andre Gide

5. "Love looks not with the eyes, but with the mind; And therefore is wing'd Cupid painted blind." —William Shakespeare

6. "Let us have faith that right makes might; and in that faith let us dare to do our duty as we understand it." —Abraham Lincoln

7. "We shape clay into a pot, but it is the emptiness inside that holds whatever we want." —Lao Tsu

8. "A great deal of intelligence can be invested in ignorance when the need for illusion is deep." —Saul Bellow

THE ALCHEMICAL
PENTAGRAM SPREAD
A Five-Card Spread

In order to explain the background for this section's spread, I should begin with a brief discussion of the alchemical philosophy of the basic elements that make up our physical world. In premodern cosmology, the world was thought to be composed of four elements—earth, air, water, and fire—along with a fifth element, spirit, with which the other four were invested, from which the other four came, and to which the other four returned.

Today our concept of the elements that make up the world is based on the atomic structure of matter, but the ancient view that everything is made up of four elements (or five, counting spirit) is still a valuable metaphor that is widely used in Western esoteric thought. In that philosophical system, these elements are often associated with characteristics as described below.[15]

Fire represents energy, will, passion, desire, libido, inspiration, growth, and enthusiasm. It is the spark of life and the will to survive, create, and procreate. The unconscious mind, intuition, emotions, and relationships are traditionally associated with water, which is also about reflection, receptivity, and imagination. Air means the things of the mind, such as thoughts, ideas, intellect, logic, reason, decisions, beliefs, and communication. It also is associated with volatility, conflict, and action. Earth is associated with the material things

---

15. Note these associations are not the definitive word on this subject. There are other valid associative schemes, but the one used in this section is the most common.

in life such as the body, resources, wealth, and commerce. It also is concerned with strength and labor, as well as security, value, and generosity. Finally, the quintessential fifth element, spirit, is associated with the more esoteric themes of morality, ethics, religion, philosophy, karma, and dharma. Also, it can represent the universal archetypes of human existence, and it is the soul or divine essence of all things.

Classification systems that describe a totality (such as the human body, the world, or the universe) in terms of discrete categories have been used as a basis for creating many Tarot spreads. For example, there are various spreads based on the twelve astrological signs, the four seasons, and the seven chakras of the human body. The five classical elements described above define another such system, and they form the basis of this section's spread, serving as inspiration for the positional definitions of its five cards. It is important to note, however, that while these definitions have worked well for my readings, this spread is highly flexible, and you may base your own positional definitions on whatever elemental associations work well for you (some alternatives are provided at the end of this section under "Alternative Spreads").

Once I had decided upon both the individual positional meanings and the underlying theme for the spread, the pattern for the cards that seemed most natural was that of a five-pointed star. Besides the fact that the pentagram (which defines the same five points as a star) is quite an obvious five-sided figure, the star is a common alchemical symbol for these five elements. Also, this pattern allowed me to present the cards in a circular path, which was intuitively satisfying. This is because it resonates with the philosophical viewpoint that our divine soul (card 1: "Spirit") descends through will, emotions, and thought (cards 2 through 4: "Fire," "Water," "Air") in order to manifest in the material world (card 5: "Earth") so that we can fulfill our divine purpose and return to the spirit of the universe (card 1).

The Alchemical Pentagram spread has a rather specialized intent. It is not one that I typically use for questions about mundane problems since usually there are better spreads for questions like, "Will my lover come back to me?" and "How can I get a promotion at work?" However, the Alchemical Pentagram spread is well suited for answering more philosophical questions such as, "What is the deeper meaning of what is happening in my life right now?" or "What is the purpose of my life?" It also works well when querents have no specific question but just want a general reading about their life.

The Spread

Begin by dealing five cards as indicated in Figure 13.

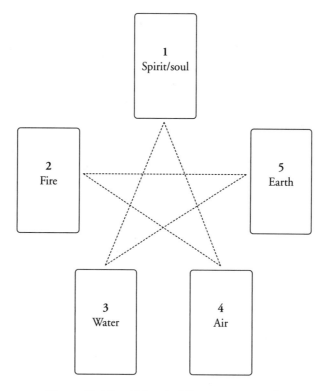

Figure 13. The Alchemical Pentagram spread.

Interpret these cards using the following positional definitions:

1. **Spirit/soul.** The divine essence of life, spirituality, psychological archetypes.

2. **Fire.** Inspiration, passion, desire.

3. **Water.** Unconscious motives, intuition, emotions, relationships.

4. **Air.** The conscious mind, ideas, beliefs, communication.

5. **Earth.** Body, resources, the material things in life.

You may, of course, refine these positional meanings based on your own interpretation of their elemental associations, or you may want to make them more specifically tailored to the circumstances of the reading at hand, as was done in the following reading.

A KnightHawk Reading with the Alchemical Pentagram Spread

Dear KnightHawk,

I have studied both science and magic, mastering much in both fields, and I have many worldly accomplishments, yet I still feel unsatisfied in my quest to find the meaning of life. How can I ever come to understand my purpose in the world? Wherein shall I find fulfillment? I would make a pact with the devil himself if he could satisfy my yearnings for such understanding, but I doubt that even he could give me that which I desire.

I am in despair. Please, can you help me find my way to salvation?

Yours most truly,
Dr. Heinrich Faust

*   *   *

Dear Dr. Faust,

Thank you for entrusting me with this deeply personal question. I have done a reading for you to see what the cards can tell us about your divine purpose and about what is going on in four essential areas of your life regarding your spiritual quest. The cards that I have laid out are the following:

1. The divine purpose of your life:
   Page of Swords

2. The passion or inspiration that is important to you at this time:
   Ace of Wands

3. Intuitive wisdom or guidance that your subconscious is offering you:
   Queen of Cups reversed

4. Ideas or concepts that you are following:
   King of Wands

5. The main source of nurturing or abundance available to you right now:
   Five of Pentacles

Let me begin by noting the elemental associations of the cards and of their positions. In this reading, we have a fire card (Wands) in the "Fire" position (card 2:

"Passion and inspiration"), a water card (Cups) in the "Water" position (card 3: "Subconscious intuition"), and an earth card (Pentacles) in the "Earth" position (card 5: "Nurturing and abundance"). The only elemental mismatch among the four mundane positions in this spread, cards 2 through 5, is the King of Wands (a fire card) that is in the "Air" position (card 4: "Ideas and concepts"). It is remarkable that we have matches in three out of four positions, so my attention is drawn to the one exception. I see in it that the mental realm is the one in which we will find your greatest misalignment with your pursuit of meaning and fulfillment.

I also want to point out that there is only one reversed card in this reading (which is card 3: "Subconscious intuition"). This implies that it is the realm of your emotions and subconscious that you are encountering the most resistance in your spiritual quest.

We shall examine the implications of these two observations further as we now turn to the messages of the individual cards in this reading. The first card, the Page of Swords, explores the divine purpose of your life. This card is about having an open mind, a thirst for knowledge and understanding, and an innocent sense of awe about the world around you. The image on this card seems to depict someone joyfully setting out to experience life fully in order to understand it. Based on these observations, I believe that this card is saying that it is through your avid desire to understand life and to find higher meaning in it that you can find your way to your divine purpose. Just be sure to keep an open mind and a willingness to experience life and learn from your experiences—your failures as well as your successes.

The next card, the Ace of Wands, discusses your guiding passions and sources of inspiration. First of all, it says that a new opportunity to explore your desires is coming into your life at this time, and it urges you to avail yourself of the intense, new experiences afforded by this opportunity. This card also reinforces the previous card's advice to savor and live your life to the fullest and to act with spontaneity. More specifically, the Ace of Wands says that your yearning for change, your willingness to explore the unknown, and even your libido can all propel you along your journey of discovery.

The Queen of Cups is a card that often indicates a loving empathy for the people around us and sensitivity to their feelings and emotions. Being reversed, however, I see that you have a resistance to these qualities—or at least to this sort of message from your subconscious mind—and your recognition of these traits will take quite some time. Thus, this card advises you to try to open up emotionally to other people and also to open yourself to your own intuitive insights. Additionally, it says that taking more time for reflection and meditation may help you with that.

Next, the King of Wands says that you are very confident about your ideas and your knowledge, so you see yourself as a mature leader in your fields of expertise. However, to some extent this may be your ego talking, which may be getting in the way of your ability to explore new challenges, to seek new knowledge, and to find true wisdom. On the other hand, the indomitable will that this card says you have should serve you well in your quest for fulfillment.

At first glance, it seems rather ironic that the Five of Pentacles should be the card to depict a source of nurturing and abundance for you. However, this card has layers of meaning that go deeper than its superficial appearance of poverty and hardship. It can indicate the voluntary release of your physical wants and needs for the sake of finding a higher, more spiritual meaning in life. With that in mind, I see that your desire to transcend your material needs—in fact, your spiritual yearning itself—can be your best source of comfort. This card also says that helping others who are in need will nurture you as much as it does them. It is through such acts of generosity that you can rise above earthly pleasures and find the spiritual understanding that you seek.

In conclusion, let us consider these five cards together in order to read the story that they tell. They say that your divine purpose will be realized through your thirst for truth and understanding. This eagerness to learn the meaning of life can be energized and driven forward by following your passions and then working to open up to your emotions until you come to a point where you have mastered those passions. It is then that you will be able to release your material needs and find fulfillment through generosity and service to others.

Thank you for requesting this reading, Dr. Faust. I hope it helps you.

Best of luck,
KnightHawk

Comments on a Reading with the Alchemical Pentagram Spread

While the oldest Faust legends are about the title character's temptation and fall from grace, Goethe's nineteenth-century treatment of the tale is about his redemption as well. That is the version I chose to use as the basis of this reading. At the beginning of Goethe's *Faust,* the scholarly Dr. Heinrich Faust is burdened with a sense of ennui despite his many achievements and accomplishments. In the depths of his depression, he makes a pact with the devil in hopes of gaining the power to discover meaning and fulfillment in his life. With the devil's help, he tries to find happiness through such means as sensual pleasures, a love affair (which ends tragically), worldly experiences, and power, but all to no avail. Finally, he refocuses his efforts, turning from the material to the spiritual, and he begins to work for the benefit of others. In the end, then, his soul is redeemed by his ceaseless striving to find spiritual truth, and the devil's scheme to win his soul fails.

Often in a Tarot reading the cards that are the most difficult to make sense of yield the greatest opportunity for understanding. In the Faust reading, it was baffling at first to see how the Five of Pentacles, with its image of poverty and illness, could be a source of nurturing and abundance. Then I remembered that before Faust summoned the devil, he had said that he would give up his earthly pleasures if, in so doing, his spiritual desires could be satisfied. Despite that statement, however, it was not until the end of the story that Faust really made such a trade. So this card revealed the final lesson that he needed to learn—that his comfort and fulfillment could be found in the voluntary renunciation of material needs in favor of helping others in greater need.

Specific Notes About Individual Positions in the Spread

POSITION ONE: THE DIVINE PURPOSE OF YOUR LIFE

A good understanding of what the card in this position says is pivotal to seeing the big picture when doing a reading with this spread. Depending on the relative importance of the spiritual aspect of the question for the reading, the other four cards should be viewed in light of what this one has to say.

For example, this factor was especially important in the reading for Faust since his question specifically addressed his pursuit of spiritual fulfillment. Thus, I interpreted cards 2 through 5 in light of the themes of inquisitiveness, education, and the exploration of new ideas, which are all inherent in the Page of Swords (card 1). Card 1 provides a place from which to start thinking about the other cards, and it allows us to view them from a perspective that may yield surprising new insights into what they mean in a particular reading. Also, considering cards 2 through 5 in light of card 1's message lends a cohesive theme to a reading using the Alchemical Pentagram spread. Of course, this does not mean that each of the other four cards in this spread will not have its own story to tell.

POSITION TWO: THE PASSION OR INSPIRATION THAT IS IMPORTANT TO YOU AT THIS TIME

The description for this position is somewhat ambiguous in order to make its use more flexible. Is the inspiration indicated by this card already recognized or actualized by the querent? If so, maybe he needs to focus his attention on it, or perhaps he should appreciate it more. On the other hand, it may be that the querent is unaware of what this card indicates. In that case, it may be important for him to discover or develop the passion implied by this card. Sometimes both perspectives of this card may be valid. In Faust's reading, for example, the Ace of Wands stressed the importance of his desire for new experiences, and it also urged him to develop more spontaneity in his life.

POSITION THREE: THE INTUITIVE WISDOM OR GUIDANCE THAT YOUR SUBCONSCIOUS IS OFFERING YOU

Since the guidance indicated by this card is from the querent's subconscious, he probably is not consciously aware of it yet. However, such intuitive insights often lurk on the periphery of our awareness, sometimes surfacing in our dreams or manifesting as nagging suspicions.

So this card's message often strikes a responsive chord, like a familiar face we cannot quite place. In Faust's case, the Queen of Cups was reversed, which emphasized his resistance to accessing the qualities it had to offer. Nevertheless, I still think he would have greeted her advice "to open up emotionally to other people and . . . to your own intuitive insights" with a response of, "Oh yeah, I guess I *should* do that. It's just hard for me." Even if a querent does deny the message of this third card, at least we have planted its seed in his conscious awareness. Then, when he is ready to listen to the advice of his subconscious mind, he will be better prepared to hear what it has to say.

POSITION FOUR: THE IDEAS OR CONCEPTS THAT YOU ARE FOLLOWING
We tend to manifest the thoughts with which we are preoccupied, including our fears as well as our hopes. So the card in this position may help explain why the querent's life is headed in a certain direction. This card also may comment on how his ideas are affecting him regarding the issue at hand; it illustrates how they are helping him or (as is often the case) how they are hindering him. For Faust, the King of Wands card indicated that he held an image of himself as an expert in various fields, and then pointed out that this self-image held him back from being open to new ideas, knowledge, and wisdom.

POSITION FIVE: THE MAIN SOURCE OF NURTURING OR ABUNDANCE AVAILABLE TO YOU RIGHT NOW
Sometimes the last card in this spread reminds the querent of all that he should be thankful for, as it provides the helpful reminder that the glass is half full, not half empty. More often, though, it suggests a source of support or comfort, either in the world around the querent or within himself. Thus, this can be the most immediately helpful card in this spread, although it may not have been so for Faust. Even though he ultimately needed to take the advice of the Five of Pentacles ("It is through . . . acts of generosity that you can . . . find the spiritual understanding that you seek"), his immediate actions suggest that he was not ready to seek the austerely spiritual comfort offered by this card at the time that he would have requested this reading.

Other Notes About This Spread

Seeing the big picture is helpful both in beginning a reading and in providing closure for it. In support of that, the following are a couple of notes that suggest ways to consider the cards in this spread as a whole versus how to understand them individually.

First, recall that each position of the Alchemical Pentagram spread is related to one of the classical elements, as are the suits in a Tarot deck.[16] Because of this, it can be an illuminating exercise to see how well the elemental associations of the cards match those of their corresponding positions. If they all match, this in itself may indicate that the querent is well aligned with his purpose. If none match, it may indicate a general misalignment in his life. Of course, this is not a hard-and-fast rule, so let your intuition guide you.

In Faust's reading, the fact that the card/position combinations matched for three out of the four mundane (i.e., nonspiritual) elements focused my attention on the one misaligned card: the fire card (King of Wands) in the air position (card 4). The fact that this card did not "fit" led me to see the King of Wands in a more problematic light than I might have otherwise. Thus, I saw that Faust's ego and overconfidence were holding him back, blocking the humility he needed in order to find true enlightenment.

A second suggestion stems from the fact that the cards in a spread often can be read together as one continuous whole. While this is true for any spread, it is an especially viable technique for this one, since these five cards address each of the classical elements. As such, they are like the pieces of a puzzle that form a complete picture when joined together. The conclusion of the reading for Faust presents an example of this way of considering the cards in the Alchemical Pentagram spread.

Alternative Spreads

The specific positional definitions used in this section's reading are by no means the only ones possible for this type of spread. For example, an Alchemical Pentagram spread may be defined as simply as this:

1. Your soulful purpose

2. What you desire

3. What you feel

4. What you think

5. What you have

---

16. The most common elemental association for the Tarot suits is: Pentacles = earth, Swords = air, Cups = water, Wands = fire, and the major arcana = spirit or soul.

However, for any particular reading using the Alchemical Pentagram spread we may tailor the positional definitions to suit the situation at hand more explicitly. In support of that effort, the following are definition suggestions for each of the five positions in this type of spread:

Position One: Spirit/Soul

- Who you really are at a spiritual level
- The path your soul is taking at this time
- Divine guidance for your problem

Position Two: Fire

- Where you need to concentrate your energy and willpower
- Your greatest source of strength, inspiration, and courage
- The driving force in your life

Position Three: Water

- The emotional aspects of your situation
- Your unconscious motivations
- How love can be a healing force in your life
- How your relationships are affecting your soulful purpose

Position Four: Air

- What you need to understand about your situation
- Beliefs and concepts that are shaping your actions
- Channels of communication you need to open

Position Five: Earth

- Resources that are available to help you
- Material concerns that are affecting you
- Your sense of self-worth

Finally, it is important to realize that the choice of positional definitions is an intuitive one that should be based on the circumstances of the reading. This is a decision that should be made before beginning a reading.

THE EXTENDED TEMPORAL SPREAD
A Five-Card Spread

The best-known three-card spread is probably the time-based Past, Present, Future spread. It is a simple and straightforward spread that works well when the querent is seeking general insights or guidance. Consequently, it is well suited for quick, informal readings, such as those one might do at a party, for example. For more complex situations or for readings for which there is more time available, a larger spread may be more appropriate. I decided to create one that was a bit more intricate, but that would retain its applicability to general situations and questions. An obvious idea, then, was to expand upon the three-card Past, Present, Future spread, giving it additional cards in order to allow for deeper and more varied insights. I wanted to maintain the universal applicability of the original spread, so I chose to split the past and future positions into two cards each (one for the near term and another for the long term), thus arriving at the spread described in this section.

The process described above is an example of how we can create a new spread based on an existing one by breaking positions in the original spread into component parts or expanding them in new directions. For the spread illustrated in this section, I used the former technique, although I also made the positional definitions more specific to the circumstances of this particular reading. Had I wanted to expand on some of the positions instead, I might have substituted "Problems" and "Advice" for the position of the "Present," for example. In fact, at the end of this section, you will find an alternative spread that uses that idea to expand upon the Extended Temporal spread.

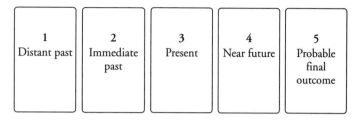

Figure 14. The Extended Temporal spread.

The Spread

Begin by dealing five cards as indicated in Figure 14.

Interpret these cards as follows:

1. **Distant past.** Things from your past that have shaped your life and set the foundation for the situation in which you now find yourself.

2. **The immediate past.** More recent influences having a direct effect on your situation.

3. **The present.** Insights into what is going on in your life right now. Clarification of your situation.

4. **Near future.** Where you currently are headed. The immediate consequences of your actions today.

5. **Probable final outcome.** The probable outcome of your current situation based on the trajectory of your life. The long-term consequences of your decisions and actions now and in the near future.

A KnightHawk Reading with the Extended Temporal Spread

Sir KnightHawk,

King Louis XV is dead, and now my husband and I are king and queen of France. The Parisians seem to love me, but there is much political intrigue in the royal court, and I fear I have more foes than friends here at Versailles. Unfortunately, my husband is

weak willed, and I am ill equipped to deal with politics and the affairs of state. How, then, will I fare as queen of France? And what do you foresee for our reign?

Her Majesty,
Marie Antoinette, Queen of France

*   *   *

Your Majesty,

I am honored by your request for a Tarot reading. I have done the following reading to examine the significant aspects of your life that are relevant to your current state of affairs: what led up to it and where you are going from here. However, I must caution you to remember that we each have a measure of control over our fate, and so any prediction may be affected by your subsequent decisions and actions.

Now, turning to your reading, the cards that I have dealt are as follows:

1. What things from your past have been significant in shaping your life?
   The Moon reversed

2. What past events are having an immediate influence on your current situation?
   The Lovers

3. What is going on in your life right now?
   Two of Swords reversed

4. Where is your life headed?
   Ten of Cups

5. What is the probable long-term forecast for your life based on current trends?
   The Tower reversed

A general first impression of this reading is that it presents quite a mixture of happiness and sadness, auspicious portents and ill omens. Along with the preponderance of major arcana cards, this indicates that you are now at a vital nexus point in your life.

Let us now discuss the specific cards individually, beginning with the Moon, a card that speaks of illusions and fears. This card tells me that your childhood, spent within the confines of a royal upbringing, left you in the dark about something—perhaps about how common people live their lives. Thus, you have illusions about life that only now are being dispelled. Although the reversed aspect of this card indicates that this influence is waning, elements of its image are echoed in the card representing the present (the Two of Swords), which tells me that these illusions still persist and will be hard to shrug off. Being next to the Lovers card, the Moon also says that you had fears and illusions about your marriage, but they, too, are diminishing now.

The Lovers card is an auspicious one that says your marriage to the dauphin, now king of France, has carried you to the level of popularity with the people of France that you have noted. It also indicates that working together, the two of you have the potential to accomplish great things. Additionally, this card may signify the union of France and Austria, which your marriage was intended to secure. In that case, this card shows that union to have gone well so far. Since this card is in the position of the immediate past, however, it indicates that perhaps the honeymoon period is now ending—either for your marriage, for your popularity with the Parisians, or for the alliance between France and Austria. How any of these conditions will develop depends on how you handle the difficult decisions you are being called upon to make at this point in your life—which brings us to the next card in this reading.

The card representing the present, the reversed Two of Swords, strikes an ominous note. For one thing, it implies that support for you as queen is shaky, and so you should be especially careful about your actions and decisions at this time. Try to be more aware of what is going on around you, and choose your path carefully. This card says that you may be safe if you can maintain your balance, however. Also, you say that you "have more foes than friends" in the royal court, but I see a different message in this card. What I see is that you have both supporters and detractors, but it is up to you to discern which is which and then to strike a balance between them. This places you in a delicate and precarious position though, and since this card is reversed, I see that striking that balance is difficult for you, or you even may be ignoring that effort. Most of all, this card indicates that compromise, tact, and diplomacy are needed at this time, and to succeed you must cultivate those qualities.

On a mundane level, the next card, the Ten of Cups, shows you and the king starting a family, which should bring you joy. This card typically is one of great happiness, but in this reading, it is flanked by troublesome cards, which seems to bring out its shadow aspects. For one thing, in the midst of the crises indicated by the cards flanking it, the scene on this card seems overly idealistic, as if it might be warning you not to get lost in a romanticized view of your life. Be realistic about your position, your family, and the friends closest to you. Also, the people depicted in this card are up in the clouds, separated from the real world. Such a feeling or attitude (i.e., of being above it all) may be what has the potential to lead you to the catastrophe of the next card.

The Tower card is a portent of both great danger and great opportunity. It denotes a situation based on a faulty foundation that is doomed to come crashing down. The opportunity in this is that you can walk away from this flawed situation before it collapses so that you can find a more realistic and stable one. Consequently, this card asks you to question your assumptions about your life. In your case, I can see one obvious question, especially since the crown of the tower is being blasted: how stable is the monarchy of France in general and your position as queen in particular? Of course, you may want to question the military, political, or financial stability of France itself as well.

It also may be valuable to relate the Tower card to the one preceding it: the Ten of Cups. Comparing the family living up in the clouds to the people falling from the Tower, I see a suggestion that your high living at court will put you in peril. Together, these two cards urge you to be more practical and to try to improve your understanding of the lives of the common people in your kingdom—the ones not living in the clouds.

There is one mitigating aspect of this last card, though. Being reversed, and in the position of a long-term forecast, I see that its manifestation will be delayed. The catastrophe it predicts will be long in coming, so there is time for you to change the future it predicts by heeding the advice of the warnings in this reading.

In conclusion, let me summarize the highlights of this reading. Your childhood kept you in the dark about life in the real world, and your marriage, which was an auspicious event, has led you to a precarious position where important decisions are needed and a delicate balancing of opposing forces is required. The near future looks bright, but its happiness may blind you to the responsibilities and problems of being queen of France, which may lead to a dangerous situation in the more distant future.

It has been an honor to do this reading for you, Your Majesty, and I pray it will prove to be of help to you.

Sincerely,
KnightHawk

Comments on a Reading with the Extended Temporal Spread

In order to shed more light on this reading, a few comments about the life of Marie Antoinette are in order. Most people know two things about this ill-fated queen: first, that when the Parisians rioted for want of bread, her response was, "Let them eat cake," and second, that she was beheaded during the French Revolution. In truth, however, only the latter happened. The quote "Let them eat cake" was a bit of slander popularly circulated during the decades leading up to the revolution, and it had been attributed to others in the French nobility prior to Marie Antoinette. Consequently, its attribution to her is highly suspect.

Although her actual callousness fell short of the vicious gossip that dogged her in the later half of her life, Marie Antoinette did have faults and shortcomings that contributed to her doom. Being the daughter of an empress (the empress of Austria, Maria Theresa), and being married to the heir to the French throne at the tender age of fifteen, she grew up with no concept of the plight and deprivations of the common people. Within the context of the revolutionary fervor of her time, then, her consequent sense of entitlement and lack of empathy for the plight of the commoners helped to seal her fate.

At the time of her husband's ascension to the throne, however, the pretty nineteen-year-old queen still enjoyed a great deal of popularity with the French people. However, taking her privilege for granted, she was extravagant and remained so even as France was beset with famine and fiscal crises. Had she been sensitive to the plight of the French people, she might have reined in her excessive spending (which, although not a significant cause of France's economic plight, was a glaring symbol of her disregard for it) and avoided being scornfully labeled "Madam Deficit." In addition, she was politically naïve and when stressed, she easily became haughty. Thus, as the years passed, she was hated and distrusted more and more, which only encouraged the defamatory gossip that exacerbated her problems.

At the beginning of this reading I informed Marie Antoinette, ". . . you are now at a vital nexus point in your life." This observation was reinforced by the occurrence of the Two of Swords—one of the quintessential decision cards in the Tarot deck—at the center of this spread. This led me to a surprising conclusion about the life of Marie Antoinette.

With her execution occurring two decades after she became queen of France, it is easy to blame Marie Antoinette's doom on her actions later in life and to minimize the effects of the actions of her youth. Yet this reading indicated that the most pivotal time of her life might have been in the early years of her reign. It was then that the need for her to seek peace and compromise within the royal court existed, and it was then that she had the opportunity to secure the trust of the people of France. With the passage of time, the idea that she was haughty, aloof, and extravagant took root and flourished. As this bad reputation became set in the minds of the French people, her popularity began to spiral downward and out of control. Eventually, everything she did was interpreted negatively until, near the end of her life, there was precious little she could do to stop her tragic fall, which the Tower card so aptly depicted.

Specific Notes About Individual Positions in the Spread

POSITION ONE: WHAT THINGS FROM YOUR PAST HAVE BEEN SIGNIFICANT IN SHAPING YOUR LIFE?

In the version of the Extended Temporal spread used in this section, I altered this position's name from "Distant past" in an effort to focus attention on the specific foundations of the querent's life that set the stage for the problems or issues she faced at the time of the reading. This is how I differentiate the first position from the next one, the "Immediate past." Typically, influences from the querent's distant past shape her life and provide a backdrop for the reading. They also provide a context in which the second card may be interpreted, since the effects on the subject of the reading noted by this first card are more general than those revealed by the card in position two.

POSITION TWO: WHAT PAST EVENTS ARE HAVING AN IMMEDIATE INFLUENCE ON YOUR CURRENT SITUATION?

The second card brings the focus of the reading closer to the problems and issues at hand, since the events or factors that it discusses are more immediate than those of the prior card. However, there is a tendency—as with any spread position that addresses the past—for us to focus on the obvious interpretations of this card (especially since querents generally assume that they already understand the past, although, in fact, they often do not). Thus, I try to explore the subtleties of the card in this position: how it comments on what led up to the present conditions of the querent's life and what it may portend for the future by its implications about the trajectory of her life.

In the case of this section's reading, an obvious interpretation of the Lovers card was that it depicted Marie Antoinette's marriage, which of course was continuing to have a great impact on her life, especially since it made her queen of France. This card also may be about unions in general and about major decisions, so I tried to see how such interpretations could have been affecting Marie Antoinette's life at the time of this reading and what advice for the future they may have offered her. More specifically, I also saw that the dark clouds gathering in the next card, the Two of Swords, were casting an ominous gloom over the cheerful image of the immediate past. Hence I told Marie Antoinette, ". . . perhaps the honeymoon period is now ending."

This raises a general comment about the interdependency of all of the cards in a spread based on a temporal theme. The comparison of time to a river may be a cliché, but it is instructive here. Like a river, the flow of time at our present location depends on the course it took upstream, and it affects its current downstream. Using that analogy, we can see the inevitability of a strong relationship between the five cards in this spread.

POSITION THREE: WHAT IS GOING ON IN YOUR LIFE RIGHT NOW?

Since the present is the stage upon which we are acting out the drama of our lives, the card in this position often holds the most potent advice in a reading with this spread. While it is true that insights into the past bring understanding of the present, for many people it is more important to release the past than to dwell upon it. After all, although we should try to understand the past, we cannot change it. On the other hand, people often focus their attention on the two future positions that follow this one. Typically they are impressed by the chance to glimpse the mysterious future and are tempted by the power inherent in foreseeing it. Granted, the power of foresight should not be minimized, but the future is mutable, whereas the present is all that we ever really have to work with. Thus, I usually find card 3 to be the crux of a reading using the Extended Temporal spread.

For Marie Antoinette in particular, the time at which this reading would have been done was indeed a crucial point in her life. The third card provided her with several important pieces of advice. It pointed out current dangers and opportunities, as well as cautions about them and advice for dealing with them.

POSITION FOUR: WHERE IS YOUR LIFE HEADED?

As noted previously, since the cards in this spread form a temporal sequence, it is important to try to see how each card may lead to the one after it or how it may be the result of the one prior to it. The Ten of Cups in position four is an excellent example of this process. I noted that the Ten of Cups typically depicts great happiness, but in this reading, it is flanked by troublesome cards, which brought out its shadow aspects. Consider that if the current conditions are precarious (as noted by the Two of Swords) and the probable outcome seems ominous (as depicted by the Tower), a card that usually depicts a happy state of affairs (the Ten of Cups) may indicate conditions that will be fleeting or illusory. We may need to explore the problematic aspects of this card as well as the more obviously happy ones.

For example, one of this card's meanings concerns a happy family. Despite the fact that the royal couple had no children in the four years of marriage prior to Louis's ascension to the throne, afterward Marie Antoinette bore four children (although only two of them survived her at the time of her execution). Thus, having children seemed an obvious interpretation of this card. Indeed, Marie Antoinette was overjoyed at finally being able to give the king children, especially an heir to the throne. However, with the childhood deaths of two children, and the tragedies that subsequently befell the entire royal family, this joy was indeed ephemeral.

I also explored a shadow aspect of this card when I told Marie Antoinette that the people depicted in the Ten of Cups seem separated from the real world, which may be what would lead her to the catastrophe of the Tower card. Generally, I would not turn to such a negative view of this card when it is neither reversed nor in a problematic position, but the flow of this spread justified this interpretation.

POSITION FIVE: WHAT IS THE PROBABLE LONG-TERM FORECAST FOR YOUR LIFE BASED ON CURRENT TRENDS?

When the card in this position bodes ill, I usually look to the preceding card (or cards) for help in explaining why the outcome looks dark and in finding advice for overcoming this dire prediction. In this case, I saw in the Ten of Cups that Marie Antoinette's "high living at court" put her in the peril predicted by the Tower card.

My interpretation of the reversed aspect of this card as indicating a delay in the manifestation of the message of this card raises an interesting point about interpreting reversals in a spread that deals specifically with the past and future. There are various ways of interpreting reversed cards, but when the card lands in a future position, I generally see the reversal as being indicative of a delay. Similarly, when it is in a position dealing with the past, I often interpret the reversal as meaning that its energy is now diminishing.

Other Notes About This Spread

It is important to remember that all five cards in this spread, when considered together, depict the trends and trajectory of the querent's life. The cards in the two "Past" positions provide the context for our understanding of the card in the "Present" position. Then all three of these cards provide the foundation for interpreting the two cards in the "Future" positions.

Alternative Spreads

As I worked on this temporal spread, I thought about the nature of time and our relationship to it. The present, which is all that we ever have, is the eternal decision point of our lives, as noted by the clichéd, but valid, saying: "Today is the first day of the rest of your life." Our lives on any given day are filled with challenges, including both the niggling aggravations of day-to-day living and the larger, ongoing dilemmas that haunt us throughout entire periods of our lives. Thus, we might want to expand the "Present" position of the three-card Past, Present, Future spread into two positions: one for the querent's current problems and one for advice about handling those problems.

If we make this change to the "Present" position, though, we arrive at an interesting quandary in defining the "Future" position: should that card reflect the probable outcome if the querent takes the offered advice, or should it be the probable outcome if she ignores that advice and continues along her current path? The most common answer seems to be to make it the probable outcome if the querent takes the offered advice, but an interesting solution is to provide two cards, one for each alternative.

As a consequence of these considerations, I arrived at the following alternative to the Extended Temporal spread used in this section's reading. This alternative spread is illustrated in Figure 15.

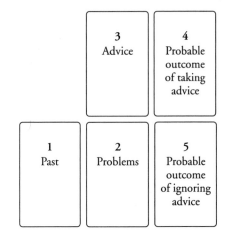

Figure 15. The Comparative Outcome spread.

Interpret the cards of the Comparative Outcome spread as follows:

1. **Past.** The important events and milestones from your past that are the foundation of your life today.

2. **Present problems.** The problems you face in your current situation.

3. **Advice for the present.** Advice about how to deal with those problems.

4. **Probable outcome of taking advice.** The probable outcome if you take the offered advice.

5. **Probable outcome of ignoring advice.** The probable outcome if you choose not to take the indicated advice and instead continue on with your life as you have been.

We can combine this spread with this chapter's Extended Temporal spread to arrive at the eight-card spread in Figure 16.

Interpret the cards in the Extended Dual Outcome spread as follows:

1. **Distant past.** Things from your past that have set the foundation for the situation in which you now find yourself.

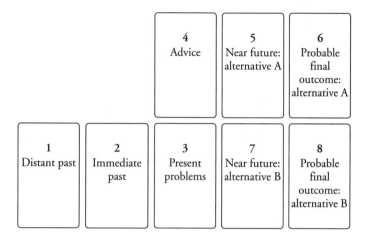

Figure 16. The Extended Dual Outcome spread.

2. **The immediate past.** Recent influences having an immediate effect on your situation.

3. **Present problems.** The problems you face in your current situation.

4. **Advice.** Advice about how to deal with those problems.

5. **Near future: alternative A.** Immediate consequences of your actions if you take the offered advice.

6. **Probable final outcome: alternative A.** Long-term consequences if you take the offered advice.

7. **Near future: alternative B.** Immediate consequences of your actions if you choose not to take the offered advice.

8. **Probable final outcome: alternative B.** Long-term consequences if you choose not to take the offered advice.

RELATIONSHIP
TRANSFORMATION SPREADS
Two Five-Card Spreads

Since relationship questions are perhaps the most prevalent type of question for Tarot readings, I have researched this subject extensively in order to increase my effectiveness as a Tarot reader. In the course of reading many books on this subject, I have found that while the details of each troubled relationship are unique, several general themes are common in most cases. With that in mind, I decided to use these themes as a basis for a Tarot spread.

Relationship disorders often result from behavior patterns that trigger the same basic problems over and over again. For example, some people typically respond to disagreements and conflicts with antagonism rather than with a desire to understand the problem and the other person. Others, conversely, are perpetual doormats in their relationships. Some people have commitment issues, while others tend to pick partners who are emotionally (or otherwise) unavailable. If the same relationship problems keep cropping up, the first place the querent should look for a solution is his or her own psychological or emotional patterns. Since these problematic patterns create such a fundamental foundation for relationship troubles, I put the position addressing them at the base of this spread.

Relationship problems also arise from our fears and from things we unconsciously do to block love in our lives. In addition, we tend to hold on to things (desires, concepts, expectations, habits, old wounds, etc.) that seem important to our egos, but that are detrimental to our relationships, and we would do well to release them. I placed the cards addressing these issues in the middle of the spread.

Finally, a mere enumeration of the querent's problems can be more depressing than helpful, so I concluded this spread with a position that talks about healing. It seemed most appropriate, from a conceptual point of view, to put this position at the top of the spread. I made it be the last card, though, partly out of a desire to end the reading on an upbeat note and partly so that its interpretation could benefit from the insights gleaned from the previous problem-oriented cards.

As I reviewed the spread that the above relationship concepts inspired, I realized that I could create two related versions of it: one to help a querent heal or improve an existing relationship and one to enable a querent to find a romantic relationship. The basic layout is the same for both, but the positional interpretations differ depending on the intention of the reading. The most notable difference occurs in the position about healing. In the Finding a Relationship spread, the relationship that the querent needs to heal in order to be able to find romance is with him- or herself.

So this section offers two sample readings: one using the spread for healing a relationship, and one using the spread for finding one. I have included readings using both spreads rather than using one and noting the other as an alternative spread because both types of readings are so very common.

The Spread

Begin by dealing five cards as indicated in Figure 17.

HEALING AND IMPROVING A RELATIONSHIP

To help the querent fix problems in an existing relationship, interpret these cards using the following positional meanings:

1. What are your problematic patterns in this relationship?

2. What are your fears in it?

3. How do you block love in it?

4. What do you need to let go of in order to make this relationship work?

5. How can you heal this relationship?

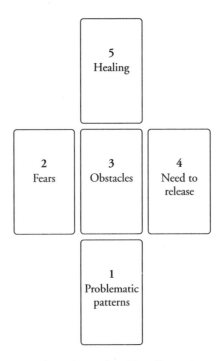

Figure 17. The Relationship Transformation spread.

FINDING A RELATIONSHIP

To help the querent find a romantic relationship, use the following positional meanings:

1. What are your patterns of resistance to having a mature and healthy relationship?

2. What do you fear about romantic relationships?

3. How do you block love in your life?

4. What do you need to let go of in order to find love?

5. How can you heal your relationship with yourself?

A KnightHawk Reading with the Relationship Transformation Spread: Fixing a Relationship

Dear KnightHawk,

That horrible husband of mine is at it again. It never fails. A pretty face catches his eye, and he can't resist chasing after her. This time it's that heifer Io.

Yet, truly I am the most beautiful of all. Why is that not enough for him? Why must he constantly shame and embarrass me? Am I doomed to suffer in this marriage forever? Please tell me, what shall I do about my husband Zeus?

Sincerely,
Hera, Queen of Olympus

*   *   *

Your Majesty,

I am honored that you have sought my advice on this delicate matter. You have asked several questions here, but I sense that beneath them all, there is one underlying question: how can you heal your marriage?

Before we begin, though, let me note that since you, not Zeus, have requested this reading, I can only ask the cards for insights about what *you* can do to heal your marriage. I cannot ask them to reveal secrets about your husband or to provide advice for him, since he is not the intended recipient of this reading.

What follows, then, is the reading that I have done for you, beginning with the cards dealt for it.

1. What are your problematic patterns in this relationship?
   Knight of Cups

2. What are your fears in this relationship?
   King of Swords

3. How do you block love in this relationship?
   The Star reversed

4. What do you need to let go of to make this relationship work?
   Two of Pentacles reversed

5. How can you heal this relationship?
   The High Priestess

First, let me make a general observation about the cards in this spread. It is interesting to note that there are cards here from every suit except Wands. This implies that in your relationship with your husband, passion or libido may be lacking, or more creativity may be needed. Of course, this does not necessarily mean that you yourself lack those qualities. Rather, it may be that your marriage lacks them, or at least it needs a positive expression of them.

As for the specific cards here, we will begin with the Knight of Cups, which is in the position that indicates recurring patterns that may be troubling your marriage. Perhaps you have a tendency to be temperamental or to get carried away by your emotional responses to events and circumstances in your marriage. Problematic patterns can cause marital difficulties to spiral out of control. In your case, it seems that your emotional reactions to your husband's infidelities drive him away from you (and toward other women) rather than draw him closer to you, which in turn leads you to have further emotional reactions. Thus, this has become a self-perpetuating problem.

On one level, the next card, the King of Swords, may represent how you see Zeus himself, and so, by extension, it may illustrate a fear of his authority. That fear may manifest itself as resentment, anger, or confrontation. Considering the stern look on this king's countenance and the fact that his arms are crossed covering his heart, this card also may indicate a fear that Zeus's heart is blocked to you. On the other hand, the King of Swords may represent an aspect of yourself, such as a need to feel in control in your relationship. In that case, this card suggests that you fear your husband's infidelity will weaken or destroy your ability to control him, or even that he no longer wants or needs you and may leave you for someone else.

The next position in this spread is concerned with how you block love in your marriage, and the first thing I see in the reversed Star is a loss of hope or a denial of it. We all need hope if we are to find solutions to our problems, but it seems that you have run out of it, which may contribute to the sense of doom that you feel in your marriage. This loss of hope in itself is enough to damage a loving relationship.

We also need hope in order to see the best in others and in our circumstances. Without it, you may see only the worst in Zeus, such as seeing him as the stern authoritarian who lacks love and tenderness that we saw in the previous card. Furthermore, without hope, you may become obsessed with the problems in your marriage and block out the good things about it, which further stifles the love in your relationship.

Besides hope, the Star card also indicates honesty and openness, as well as peace and serenity. Being reversed, though, it suggests that you might be able to unblock the love in your marriage by being more open and honest with your husband about how you feel. For example, you might tell him that you feel hurt and betrayed when he is unfaithful. Perhaps, however, you first need to be honest with yourself about how you feel. In any case, try to express your openness and honesty with the calm serenity that this card illustrates.

Before moving on to the next card, let us look at yet another message from the Star card that may be helpful in unblocking the course of love in your marriage. You state that you are "the most beautiful of all," but in its reversed aspect, the Star card suggests that deep down you doubt your true inner grace and charm. When such doubts are unconscious it is hard to overcome them, and so they can have a very unsettling effect on a relationship. They may be disrupting the peace and tranquility of your marriage, or they may be the reason that your husband's infidelity wounds you as much as it does.

There are a couple of aspects of the Two of Pentacles that are especially relevant to the issue of what you need to release: playfulness and balance. First, the Two of Pentacles, being reversed, indicates a resistance to indulging in play, fun, and whimsy. Perhaps if you can let go of that resistance, you will be able to revitalize your marriage, so try not to take everything quite so seriously. This does not mean that marriage is frivolous or that infidelity is not a serious matter. Instead, this is where the aspect of balance comes into play. The reversal of the Two of Pentacles says that there is an imbalance in your approach to your marriage that may be corrected by a little more playfulness and humor and a bit less severity and gravity.

The final card in this spread, the High Priestess, suggests how you may heal your marriage. This card symbolizes the intuitive wisdom that comes from listening to the quiet voice inside us. Significantly, this is in direct opposition to a problematic pattern that the Knight of Cups indicated (letting your emotions carry you away) and to the fear implied by the King of Swords (the fear that you are not in control of your marriage). So the next time you become jealous of your husband, don't let your emotions control your actions and drive you to wreak vengeance on everyone involved. Instead, find a place of peace, calm, and centeredness within yourself where you can hear the quiet advice of your intuition. Similarly, this card advises you to seek a balance between severity and mercy in your responses to your marital problems. There is a time and a place for each, and too much of either may be injurious to your marital bliss.

Another important aspect of the High Priestess card is that of the mysteries of femininity. Consequently, it urges you to access and capitalize on your own feminine mystique in order to enhance your allure to Zeus and to bring some enchantment back into your marriage. At the same time, the High Priestess, which sometimes is seen as a virginal ideal, may represent the self-confidence that you can find outside of the context of your marriage. Therefore, this card recommends that you rely more on yourself than on your husband or on your marriage for your sense of worth. This will allow you to maintain a more peaceful state, even when problems do arise in your marriage.

In summary, I see two major themes running through this reading. One is a need to moderate your reactions to your husband's philandering, and the other is a need for an improved self-image. This reading points out the adverse effects of harsh, emotional responses to Zeus's mistakes in this marriage, and it offers the alternatives of serenity, humor, and intuitive wisdom. It also suggests that you try to realize and make better use of your inner grace and charm, and it recommends that you find an independent sense of self-worth that is not defined by your marriage.

Thank you for requesting this reading, my lady. I hope it helps you.

Bright blessings,
KnightHawk

Comments on a Reading with the Relationship Transformation Spread

It is ironic that Hera, whose married life may have been the most troubled of any of the gods in the Greek pantheon, was the patroness of marriage, but mythology is littered with such seeming inconsistencies. Perhaps, however, Hera's marriage was merely an archetypal representation of those of her unfortunate mortal suppliants. Or maybe her problems assured her followers that she would understand and have sympathy for their heartaches over an unfaithful spouse, since Zeus was the personification of infidelity. In fact, the tales of his sexual escapades were the basis of many a Greek myth. Io, Europa, Leto, Leda, and Semele are some of the more notable names on the extensive list of his sexual conquests.

In most cases, Hera wreaked vengeance upon her rivals with unmitigated fury, regardless of how unwilling or unwitting they may have been in the affair. However, if her intention was to put an end to her husband's philandering, she failed spectacularly. Her efforts drove him to use deceit and trickery to try to cover his tracks, but they failed to improve his sense of fidelity. As a consequence, Hera was perpetually unhappy, jealous, and quarrelsome, which exacerbated her marital problems and made life miserable for everyone else involved as well. Not even the innocent progeny of Zeus's illicit affairs were safe from Hera's persecution, which is another irony given that she was also the guardian of children.

Specific Notes About Individual Positions in the Spread

POSITION ONE: WHAT ARE YOUR PROBLEMATIC PATTERNS IN THIS RELATIONSHIP?
It is important to note that this first position is not merely about problems, it is about problematic *patterns*. This is a significant distinction because troubles may come and go, but as long as dysfunctional patterns of behavior exist, they will continue to create problems in a relationship. As noted in Hera's reading, such patterns often create self-perpetuating

problems that can spiral out of control. Thus, as we interpret the card in this position, we should look for patterns of behavior that repeatedly cause and exacerbate the querent's relationship troubles.

POSITION TWO: WHAT ARE YOUR FEARS IN THIS RELATIONSHIP?

A querent's fears may masquerade as anything from hate to indifference, or from antagonism to withdrawal. Since fear can be so hard to recognize for what it is, finding the message of the second card in this spread can be a challenge sometimes. So in order to interpret this card, it helps to consider what difficulties it may represent, then ask how fear might explain or underlie those problematic circumstances or characteristics.

In addition, it is important to be aware of the diversity of fears possible within a relationship. A querent may be afraid of the other person's behavior, or she may fear her own actions or reactions in the relationship. She may fear something about the relationship itself, such as what it means or where it is headed, or she may be afraid of the influence of outside circumstances. Also, fears may be real and well founded, or they may be completely imaginary and without substance. Usually, though, they lie somewhere between those two extremes.

We should keep in mind all of these considerations when working with the card in this position. To do this, we may ask questions like these: In what form is the querent's fear manifesting? What is the cause of her fear? How real is it?

POSITION THREE: HOW DO YOU BLOCK LOVE IN THIS RELATIONSHIP?

While recognizing our fears may be a challenge, owning up to how we block love can be harder still. Although we may be quick to see how the other person in a relationship blocks his or her love, we hate to admit that we block our love too, but we do, each in our own unique way. However, the purpose of card 3 is not to find fault and place blame. Instead, it should be used to show the querent how blocking love is detrimental to her relationship, and it should address this issue with an eye toward solving this problem.

POSITION FOUR: WHAT DO YOU NEED TO LET GO OF TO MAKE THIS RELATIONSHIP WORK?

The first three cards in this spread focus primarily on problems and obstacles in the querent's relationship. Now, with the fourth card, we begin to turn our attention more toward advice and solutions.

The challenge in working with the card in position four is that just the prospect of letting go of something, no matter what it is, can scare a querent. But this card will not ask her to abandon anything that is positive or valuable to her well-being, such as her basic right to be treated fairly or to be safe from harm. Instead, the card in this position may ask her to release something that wounds her relationship or that impedes its repair or growth. For example, it may suggest that she should let go of illusions about her relationship, requirements that unnecessarily stress it, or bad habits that cause conflict in it.

In Hera's case, she was asked to release her resistance to "indulging in play, fun, and whimsy." Indeed, her approach to dealing with her husband's infidelity was completely humorless, and the grim severity of her jealousy drove him to guile and secrecy, a result that was counterproductive since it seemed to increase the thrill of the game for him. Thus, the reversed Two of Pentacles suggested that more fun in their marriage might have satisfied Zeus's need for sport in his amorous adventures. Additionally, a sense of humor may have helped Hera cope with her marital problems with less anxiety. Consequently, what this card asked Hera to release was merely her resistance to something that could improve both her marriage and her ability to deal with its problems.

POSITION FIVE: HOW CAN YOU HEAL THIS RELATIONSHIP?
The message of the final card in this spread builds upon what we learned from the preceding cards, and so it is the climax of a reading with the Relationship Transformation spread. Prior cards discussed the obstacles in the querent's relationship—problematic patterns, fears, and blockages—and may have offered some suggestions for overcoming them, but advice for healing this relationship is what card 5 is all about. Its interpretation may stand alone, but usually it is applicable to the obstacles enumerated previously in the reading as well. In Hera's reading, for example, the advice of the High Priestess was applied to the difficulties illustrated by the Knight of Cups and the King of Swords, but it also examined other dimensions of Hera's marriage, offering guidance in those areas too.

Other Notes About This Spread
Primarily, I use this spread for readings about romantic relationships. However, it is also applicable to troubled platonic relationships, such as those with friends, family members, or coworkers. In either case, the focus of the reading should be on the querent herself rather than on seeking to reveal secrets about or offer advice to someone who is not present for the reading. This is true for several reasons, but mostly it is due to the fact that

the querent can only change herself and not anyone else. While this guidance applies to any Tarot reading, it is especially important to keep it in mind during a relationship reading because it is in such readings that querents are most apt to ask us to use the Tarot for psychic eavesdropping.

Out of concern for this problem, the Relationship Transformation spread was designed so that the cards in each position would specifically talk about the querent. For example, card 1 asks, "What are your problematic patterns in this relationship?" rather than, "What problematic patterns are operating in this relationship?" The latter version might lead us to explore the shortcomings of the querent's partner, but the former focuses on what the querent can reasonably hope to control: herself.

All of this is not to say that nothing about the other person in the querent's relationship will be revealed in the course of a reading with this spread. It is just that our intention should be to examine the pertinent aspects of the querent's life, since she is the one who has requested a reading and she is the only person she can change. Where the universe takes the reading from there, however, is a matter for its greater wisdom.

Another KnightHawk Reading with the Relationship Transformation Spread: Finding a Relationship

Dear KnightHawk,

Although I am a successful young man in the prime of life, some time ago my fiancée broke off our engagement. Since then I have found no one suitable for marriage. It is true that my career has greatly occupied my time of late, but even so, I cannot understand why I seem destined for bachelorhood. What must I do to find a wife?

Yours truly,
Ebenezer Scrooge

*   *   *

Dear Mr. Scrooge,

Thank you for asking me to help you with your problems with your love life. There are various factors that may be working against you at this time, so I have used a spread that specifically examines some of the more common ones. This will help us see what you can do to bring a loving relationship into your life.

The cards I dealt for you are the following:

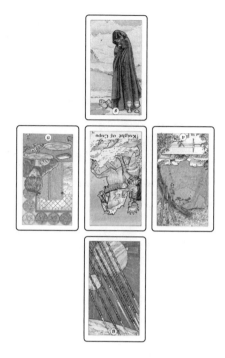

1. What are your patterns of resistance to having a mature and healthy relationship?
   Eight of Wands

2. What do you fear about romantic relationships?
   Eight of Pentacles reversed

3. How do you block love in your life?
   Knight of Cups reversed

4. What do you need to let go of in order to find love?
   Four of Swords reversed

5. How can you heal your relationship with yourself?
   Five of Cups

The first card in this spread, the Eight of Wands, discusses the patterns of resistance that sabotage your relationships. This card can indicate things like expansion and swift movement, and what I see in it here is that you are easily carried away by your desires. However, rather than being about romantic passions, in this case I think it signifies career issues, an interpretation that is reinforced by the other Eight card in this reading (the adjacent Eight of Pentacles, which is about work). Thus, the Eight of Wands implies that by being carried away by your passion for your career, you continually resist either getting into or building upon your romantic relationships. This does not mean that you have to choose between romance and career, but rather that you should recognize that your driving desire to expand your business pursuits interferes with your love life. It is only when you grasp this fact that you will be able to change this pattern of behavior.

The fears described by the next card, the reversed Eight of Pentacles, are closely related to the resistance explained by the Eight of Wands. The most obvious interpretation of the reversed Eight of Pentacles is that you fear that romance will impede or hinder your work. Another possibility, though, is that you fear that finding and maintaining a relationship will require too much work.

In some way or another we all do things that block love in our lives. The reversed Knight of Cups says that you block love by not recognizing, accepting, or appreciating romance when it rides into your life, possibly because you have your nose to the grindstone at work, as depicted in the Eight of Pentacles. It also implies that you resist acting upon your own feelings, fearing that they will take control and carry you away.

The next card talks about things in your life that do not serve you well as you look for love, and consequently that you would do well to release from your life. The Four of Swords is a card of introspection as well as of rest and recuperation. Being reversed, it indicates a resistance to introspection, so releasing that resistance can help you to find love. Thus, this card urges you to try to understand yourself better. You will need to find time and a quiet place for this though, which may require some rest and even a retreat from the rigors of your work for a while. As a result, this card also asks when was the last time you took a vacation, and it suggests that maybe it is time to take one now.

The first thing that struck me about the Five of Cups as I laid out the cards for this reading was the black cloak of mourning worn by the figure in this card. What I see in this is that your sorrow has driven you further into your work in order to escape your pain. This also may be why you deny your feelings, because doing so keeps them from being hurt again. Therefore, the Five of Cups says that a mantle of sorrow hides the real you from others. Even worse, though, it hides you from yourself. Also, you may wear this somber cloak to protect yourself from further pain and loss, but it stifles you and keeps you from enjoying your life.

This card is about mourning a loss, and it recommends that you resolve your grief about that loss. However, it also says that while grieving is important, there comes a time when you must stop brooding and move on with your life. It is only then that you will reclaim the things of value that remain in your life, and this can help you heal your relationship with yourself.

This leads us to another important aspect of this card: the two cups that remain standing and thus indicate that all is not lost. Interpreting these cups by the color of their rims (red and green), I see in them an indication that in order to heal your relationship with yourself, you need to recognize and appreciate your emotional vitality and passion. This advice corresponds well with what the Four of Swords said about being more introspective, for that process can help you understand your emotional self better.

In conclusion, the main message that I see in this reading is that you have focused your attention and efforts on your career at the expense of working on romance—or on understanding yourself better—since your business is a pursuit that is emotionally safe for you. Therefore, if you can come to grips with past emotional pains and complete your grieving process for them, you should be able to move on with your love life.

Thank you for requesting this reading, Mr. Scrooge. I hope it helps you.

Best of luck,
KnightHawk

Comments on a Second Reading with the Relationship Transformation Spread

Charles Dickens's *A Christmas Carol* is perhaps the best-known Christmas story in the English language and its main character, Scrooge, is an excellent subject for a Tarot reading. This is due to the fact that Scrooge has a very disturbed life with very little understanding why it is so. On the other hand, as the tale illustrates, he has a strong potential for redemption.

For the above reading, the situation I used was based on an event in Scrooge's early adult life. One of the scenes that the Ghost of Christmas Past showed Scrooge took place when he was a young man and his fiancée released him from their engagement. In doing so, she told him that another idol—a golden one—had taken her place in his heart, which revealed that monetary concerns had already gained ascendancy over love in Scrooge's life. Perhaps this was the result of the childhood pains previously shown to him by this particular Christmas spirit. This reading echoes the concerns of Scrooge's fiancée—that his career had become the center of his life—but it goes on to give him some guidance as well.

Specific Notes About Individual Positions in the Spread

The positions in the Finding a Relationship version of this section's spread have meanings similar to the corresponding ones in the Fixing a Relationship version that was used in Hera's reading. However, the specific focus in this variation creates some differences in those interpretations, which will be explored here.

Position One: What Are Your Patterns of Resistance to Having a Mature and Healthy Relationship?

Some people avoid making commitments, while others make them and break them with complete abandon. Some people are too shy to meet other people in the first place, while others seem to meet and fall in love with someone every time they turn around. For each person who cannot establish or hold on to a long-term relationship, there is a reason for his failure that is unique to him, and that reason generally involves a dysfunctional pattern of behavior that sabotages his efforts.[17]

As in the Fixing a Relationship version of this spread, this first position is about more than just a particular problem that the querent is having at the moment. Instead, it describes a problematic pattern that he repeats in most, if not all, of his relationships. Thus, the problem illustrated here probably is deeply rooted in the querent's psyche, so it may be hard to correct. However, if the querent can address this issue, he will go a long way toward solving his relationship troubles.

Position Two: What Do You Fear About Romantic Relationships?

Our fears are often the biggest obstacles to finding and keeping a positive relationship, and the types of fears that block romance are as varied as those noted for the correspond-

---

17. Note that I am not including here those people who are not in a long-term relationship because they prefer to remain single. Such people would not be seeking this type of a Tarot reading anyway.

ing position in the Fixing a Relationship version of this spread. For example, there are people who fear a loss of freedom, who are afraid to risk rejection or abandonment, or who fear that a relationship will interfere with their career. Also, as noted for the prior version of this spread, these fears may masquerade as any of a variety of difficult modes of behavior, and they may or may not be reasonable or justified. Again, this is important to keep in mind when interpreting the card in this position. In addition, we also must realize that a querent may be reluctant to acknowledge that he fears something that he professes to want.

POSITION THREE: HOW DO YOU BLOCK LOVE IN YOUR LIFE?

Some people, no matter how often they insist that they want a romantic relationship, seem to find ways to keep love at arm's length. Instead of trying to see what they are doing wrong, they typically blame fate or their ex-partners. In extreme cases, they come to blame, or even hate, all women or all men, whichever the case may be. Consequently, the message of the card in position three can be a hard sell because besides being unaware of his problems, the querent also may resist acknowledging them. Of course, just as when we use the Fixing a Relationship version of this spread, the primary focus of this card should be on solving the querent's problem rather than on placing blame for it. The more we can do that, the more the querent will find this card's message to be accessible and acceptable.

POSITION FOUR: WHAT DO YOU NEED TO LET GO OF IN ORDER TO FIND LOVE?

As with the other version of this spread, the card in position four will not ask the querent to let go of things that are valuable to his well-being or that are a positive influence in his life. Rather, it will show him something that he clings to (whether out of fear, habit, or a mistaken sense of worth) but that he needs to release in order to find and keep a meaningful relationship. This advice may be about something specific that he needs to do right now in order to find love, or it may indicate something he needs to rid himself of in order to hold on to a relationship when he does find one. For example, in Scrooge's reading, this card was more about what he needed to do to find love, but the change it advocated also could help him maintain a relationship if and when one came into his life.

POSITION FIVE: HOW CAN YOU HEAL YOUR RELATIONSHIP WITH YOURSELF?

When a querent wants to know how to find romance, he first needs to be sure that he has a healthy relationship with himself. After all, how can he love someone else if he cannot love himself? If he does not love himself, won't he expect that other people will find him to be unlovable as well?

So this final card may try to help the querent see and understand himself better, for with understanding comes empathy. It may reveal some of his more valuable characteristics so he can appreciate himself more and thereby see why someone else might find something in him to love. Or it may reveal how the querent blocks his love of himself. In any case, the ultimate concern of this card is to help the querent love himself more honestly and unconditionally.

In Scrooge's reading, the advice of the reversed Five of Cups included some cautionary notes, such as the observation that while his somber attitude might protect his feelings, it also stifles him and muffles his enjoyment of life. It is interesting, then, to see how starkly this card depicts the Scrooge that was to come: an unhappy man closed off from the world of humanity around him.

Other Notes About This Spread

The key cards in this spread are the first one and the last one. Card 1 introduces the querent's fundamental problems in finding and holding on to a relationship, and this establishes the theme for the entire reading. In Scrooge's case, the Eight of Wands said that his basic problem was that his enthusiasm and passion for his career carried him away—and away from love. Typically, the concerns indicated by card 1 then influence the interpretations of the next three cards in the spread. For Scrooge, card 2 said that he feared romance would interfere with his work, card 3 suggested that keeping his nose to the grindstone kept him from seeing romance when it rode into his life, and card 4 recommended a vacation from work in order to allow him to reflect upon his life.

The last card, card 5, concludes the reading with suggested solutions, which reflect back upon the problems noted in the prior cards. In Scrooge's reading, the Five of Cups talked about his unresolved grief and how it cloaked and numbed his feelings. This message was then applied to card 2 by noting that sorrow had driven Scrooge deeper into his work, card 3 by explaining that he denied intimate relationships in order to protect his wounded feelings, and card 4 by suggesting that introspection could lead to the discovery of his emotional vitality that he needed.

Finally, acknowledging the importance of cards 1 and 5 also helps us tie together the whole reading and present the querent with a succinct summary of it, as was done for Scrooge in his reading.

THE LOVERS CARD SPREAD
A Nine-Card Spread

One day as I was working with the Lovers card from the *World Spirit Tarot,* I was struck by its wealth of symbolism and the orderly manner in which those symbols are laid out in the card. The more I meditated on this card, the more I was inspired to create a spread for relationship readings based on its imagery.

6 THE LOVERS

To begin the process, I identified the essential symbolic elements of the card. Along its left side, running from top to bottom, we find a Chinese goddess named Kuan Yin, several roses, and a cherub pointing one finger up at the heavens and one down toward the earth. On the right, we can see the demigod Pan, several lilies, and a cherub clapping his hands in delight. In the middle of the card, two lovers embrace under a radiant sun.

The next step was to consider what these symbols meant to me. To do this, I used my own understanding of their meanings as well as some guidance from the booklet that comes with the *World Spirit Tarot* deck. One figure whose symbolism was not immediately obvious was Kuan Yin, but the booklet's description of her as being "peaceful" worked well for this spread. Most of the meanings that I used for the other symbols are commonly known and accepted, but two of them bear some explanation. First, although lilies generally are seen as representing purity, the *World Spirit Tarot* booklet attributes clarity to them. However, considering that clarity can mean purity of understanding, I used it. As for the sun, there are many meanings associated with it, but its appearance and location in this card reminded me of the angel on the Rider-Waite-Smith (RWS) version of the Lovers, which led me to see the sun as representing divine will.

The positional meanings for this new spread then grew out of my understanding of the symbols on this Lovers card, and the shape of the layout reflects the arrangement of those symbols on that card. Indeed, this final step of arranging the positions was relatively straightforward except that I had a choice in the placement of the cards representing the other and self. I deliberately put the other before self because doing so in a relationship is the best way to appreciate, nurture, and heal it.

The resulting spread, which is illustrated and explained below (see Figure 18), works well for readings about improving or healing a relationship. Note that it has a very positive slant, and the decision to use it is, of course, an intuitive call. If there seem to be fundamental or pathological problems in a relationship, another spread may be more appropriate (see, for example, the Relationship Transformation spread) or professional counseling may be recommended. However, if the problems do not seem that bad, or if the querent's question about her relationship is fairly general, this spread will facilitate a reading that will help bring it health, vitality, and harmony by focusing on what is right, beautiful, and beneficial about the relationship. Often that is what we really need to know or concentrate on about our relationships.

The Spread

Begin by dealing nine cards as indicated in Figure 18.

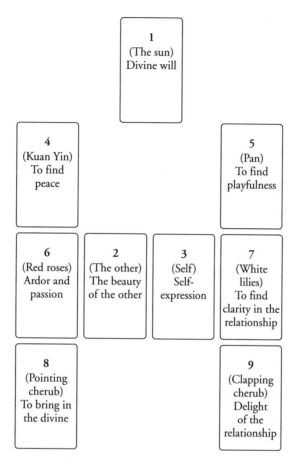

Figure 18. The Lovers Card spread.

Interpret these cards as follows:

1. What is the divine will in this relationship?

2. How can you increase your appreciation of the best attributes of the other person?

3. How can you express yourself in this relationship?

4. How can you find peace in this relationship?

5. Where can you find playfulness in this relationship?

6. What do you need to know about the ardor and passion in this relationship?

7. How can you see this relationship more clearly?

8. How can the two of you bring the divine into this relationship?

9. What is the delight in this relationship?

A KnightHawk Reading with the Lovers Card Spread

Dear KnightHawk,

Yesterday, my father married me to a man who is a lunatic. Some call me a shrew, but this man is a complete barbarian! Dressed in the most uncouth manner and behaving like a boor, Petruchio, my so-called husband, was late for our wedding. Then he would not stay for the wedding feast, but hurried us back to his home, fighting with me the whole way.

Now that we have arrived, he has found fault with everything here, including our food, so that I have had nothing to eat, I have had no rest, and I am miserable. He does all this whilst professing the utmost concern for my well-being, but he is killing me with this "kindness."

What am I to do with such a miserable lout? How can I survive such a dreadful marriage?

Yours,
Katherine Minola

*   *   *

Dear Katherine,

Thank you for requesting my help at this difficult time in your marriage. I have done a reading about your marriage to help you see how it may be saved and perhaps even transformed into something wonderful. First, though, here are the cards that I dealt for you:

1. What is the divine will in this relationship?
   The Hanged Man

2. How can you find appreciation for the best attributes of your husband?
   Five of Pentacles

3. How can you express yourself in this relationship?
   Knight of Wands reversed

4. How can you find peace in this relationship?
   The Hermit reversed

5. Where can you find playfulness in this relationship?
   Page of Pentacles

6. How can you ignite the ardor and passion in this relationship?
   Nine of Wands

7. How can you see this relationship more clearly?
   Judgement

8. How can you both bring the divine into this relationship?
   The Empress

9. What is the delight in this relationship?
   The Devil

Let me begin with a few general observations about these cards. First of all, it is noteworthy that there are five major arcana cards in your spread. This implies that your marriage is a significant milestone in your life, and even more importantly, that there may be an important spiritual lesson in what you are experiencing right now. On the other hand, the fact that there are only two reversed cards says that your situation may not be as difficult as you think. Also, the fact that the only minor arcana cards are Wands and Pentacles says that your problems are based on issues of will and practicality more than on mental or emotional ones.

Now let's look at the individual cards here one by one.

The Hanged Man says that the problems you face in this relationship present some opportunities for you to learn a few things. First, it urges you to try to see things from another perspective. Being able to understand another person's point of view is always a challenge in a relationship, but it is particularly so when two people have very different temperaments and perspectives, as this reading indicates is the case for you and Petruchio. In addition, this card suggests that you learn to release your need for control in your life and for control of those around you. Try to see if you can surrender yourself to the flow of circumstances sometimes. This card also indicates the kind of unconditional love that enables us to make sacrifices for the good of another person, and this indicates another spiritual lesson of this marriage.

Remember, however, that this card is about the divine will for this relationship, not just for you. Thus, for example, conflict between you and Petruchio is an opportunity for both of you to grow in your willingness to consider each other's viewpoints and to make sacrifices for each other. Consequently, this card may suggest that in his strange behavior, Petruchio actually may be making sacrifices for the greater good of your marriage.

The next card, the Five of Pentacles, discusses how you can see and appreciate your husband's best attributes and characteristics. This card's image of two paupers left out in the snow and cold seems rather dire, but within the context of this reading, I see in it encouragement to stick with Petruchio "for better or for worse." You both have your problems and shortcomings, but if you each try to appreciate what the other has to offer, and if you can work together, then you should be able to find a place of peace and beauty, as depicted in this card by the lovely stained-glass window. On a more literal level, though, I see that there may be hidden benefits or value behind the deprivations that you are enduring right now (i.e., a lack of food and rest), so try to see through them to understand how Petruchio may be acting out of love and concern for you.

In the next card, we see how you can express yourself within this relationship. Being reversed, the Knight of Wands indicates a need to tone down an impulsive, hot-tempered nature. In relating to your husband, try for a bit more patience and careful consideration before you speak and act. This does not mean that you need to douse the flames of your passions, just that you would do well to express them more maturely. Try to redirect your energies toward more creative endeavors, perhaps ones that are more supportive of your new marriage.

From what you have said, it seems that finding peace in this relationship may be particularly challenging for you, so you may find the message of the next card to be especially valuable. The primary message that I see in the reversed Hermit is that to find peace in this relationship, you must first find it inside yourself. How can you do that? A possibility is that the old man depicted in this card may represent your father, and perhaps you feel betrayed or abandoned by him. In that case, this card urges you to stop holding on to such feelings in order to find the internal peace that will lead to peace in your relationship. Also, that sense of being left out in the cold by your father has made you feel alone, and this card indicates that now you have a chance to end that loneliness. It urges you to stop trying to make it on your own and to allow someone else (like Petruchio) into your life.

The Page of Pentacles suggests that you can find playfulness in your marriage through an appreciation of the simple things in life. Fun need not depend upon expensive pursuits, so the two of you should be able to find a sense of play in everyday things and through a sense of openness and wonder about each other. In addition, this card sometimes can be an indication of the birth of a child. Due to the coincident appearance in this spread of the Empress (which is a card that may signify pregnancy), the Page of Pentacles could promise you a child, which will bring playfulness into your lives as well.

The somber image on the Nine of Wands makes it hard at first to see how this card could propose a way to stoke the fires of passion in your marriage. However, recalling the emotional wounds suggested by the nearby Hermit card, the Nine of

Wands may mean that you have become defensive and are using your fiery temper as a barrier to keep people from getting too close to you. One of the lessons of this card is that you should learn from past adversity rather than become embittered by it, and in so doing, you can grow in strength and character. Thus, this card says that you already have the passion and ardor that this relationship requires, but it also recommends that you try to find a more mature way to express your passion, which reinforces the message of the reversed Knight of Wands.

An obvious way to interpret the next card, Judgement, is to consider its title literally. In that case, it says that careful judgment will enable you to see this relationship more clearly. Delving deeper into this card, however, I see advice to move beyond the restrictive parochial views and concepts that you grew up with. Open yourself to new revelations so you may see your present circumstances anew. In fact, if you reassess your life up to this point, you may be able to see a whole new life for yourself in this marriage. Therefore, you may find in it a sense of renewal and a new lease on life.

The next card, the Empress, says that your expression of love for each other and your nurturing of and providing for each other will imbue your marriage with spirituality and call the divine into it. Of course, you only have control over your own actions, but being in this spread position, which asks how you *both* can bring the divine into your marriage, this card holds the promise that Petruchio has the capacity to be loving and nurturing too. Consequently, you may want to interpret his present actions in that light. On another level, as noted above in our discussion of the Page of Pentacles, the Empress sometimes indicates pregnancy and motherhood, so maybe it will not be long before you have a child, which may be another way that the divine can enter into your marriage.

The last card, the Devil, is another that seems hard to figure out, but upon careful examination, we can see just how appropriate it is here. First, let's look at the actual image on this version of the Devil card. Here, two figures—a man and a woman—are trying to pull a treasure chest in opposite directions. This implies that the delight in this relationship actually may arise out of the struggles and conflicts between the two of you as you both try to assert yourselves and your needs. How might that be delightful? Well, it seems that you have very high spirits and Petruchio can be rather adamant or even stubborn. This is a combination that may cause problems sometimes (like now), but it also promises that there will never be a dull moment in your marriage. If you can come to understand and deal with each other better, that excitement can turn into delight.

There are a couple of completely different aspects of this card that may prove enlightening as well. One of the traditional meanings of the Devil card is mirth and humor, so it may be advising you to find delight in your marriage by acting devilish sometimes, although with good humor, of course. In addition, though, the Devil card may have another, darker comment. It seems to be a warning not to let your passions and desires get out of control or else they could turn the delight in this relationship into a trap.

Now let's see what additional insights we can get from considering some clusters of cards within this spread. First, we will consider the four cards that run across the center of the spread and that depict the two of you within the context of your relationship. These are cards 6, 2, 3, and 7.

Since both the Judgement card and the suit of Wands are associated with fire, there is a lot of passion in all of these cards except for card 2, the card that talks about your appreciation of Petruchio. This card, being in the suit of Pentacles, is associated with earth, and thus with things like material concerns, strength, and dependability. This elemental contrast between fire and earth advises that your relationship with Petruchio will be improved if you try to act less willful with him while you also try to focus more on his practical assets, such as his ability to protect and provide for you.

Next, compare just cards 2 and 3, which are about Petruchio and you. Here we see that his association with an earth card says that he is strong and well grounded (although maybe a bit stubborn), while your fire card says that you are willful and high spirited. It is important, then, to keep that contrast in mind as you try to understand your relationship and work to reconcile your disparate approaches to it.

In light of these comments about Petruchio, I can see another facet of the Nine of Wands that is important in this reading. This card has an element of patience, and through his earth association as noted above, Petruchio probably does too. Consequently, the Nine of Wands suggests that you may need to wait a while for the romantic ardor of this relationship to ignite. It will come, but in its own time.

Now let us look at three cards that create a triangle that spans the length and breadth of this spread: cards 1, 8, and 9. The Hanged Man and the Empress (cards 1 and 8) share a common element: love. The Hanged Man indicates an unselfish love that is willing to sacrifice for others, and often the Empress is concerned with marital love. Both of these cards are in positions about the relationship between the divine and your marriage, so I see that the spiritual aspect of your marriage depends upon the giving and unselfish love that both of you can bring to it. As for card 9, I include it in this cluster because the delight of a relationship can be both an expression of your spirituality and a divine gift. In the context of this cluster of cards, then, the Devil card depicts a great treasure in your relationship—but you two must work together in a spirit of love and compromise in order to access that good fortune. If you act at cross-purposes, that treasure will remain inaccessible.

In summary, this reading urges both of you to recognize and appreciate your differences and to strive to understand each other. Such an effort will help your marriage—and both of you as well—to grow and thrive, although it may call for some sacrifices, a bit of work on self-improvement, and a strong sense of humor. Besides compensating for your differences, though, enjoy them too, for they add spice to your relationship.

Ultimately, then, this reading is encouraging about your ability to attain the joy of a happy marriage. Thank you for requesting this reading, and I hope it helps you.

Best of luck,
KnightHawk

Comments on a Reading with the Lovers Card Spread

The message and meaning of Shakespeare's play *The Taming of the Shrew* usually is seen as a mere reflection of its title. It makes it seem to be a simple tale in which Petruchio tames the shrewish Kate, as if he were breaking in a wild horse. Actually, the analogy given in act 4, scene 1 is that he plans to tame her in the same way that falcons are tamed: through hunger and fatigue.[18]

It was due to this popular conception of *The Taming of the Shrew* that I hesitated to use it for a KnightHawk reading, wondering if it really is a bit misogynistic. However, when I reviewed the play to see if there might be something in it that could provide material for a reading, I found sufficient cause to view Kate sympathetically. I saw that she was not really a shrew, but merely a willful young woman embittered by jealousy of

---

18. Perhaps if the Nine of Pentacles, which includes a hooded falcon, had come up in this reading I might have agreed with that view of this play.

her more popular sister and by resentment toward her father who favored that sister. Similarly, there was reason to think that Petruchio acted out of love for this spirited young woman, as well as out of a sense of self-interest, of course. Indeed, his actions hastened and guided her maturation into womanhood, a transformation that seems to have benefited both of them.

Thus, I was able to see a depth of character in both Petruchio and Kate that I hope came through in Kate's reading. For example, the interpretation of the Devil card as including mirth and humor supports a more benign than usual view of Kate's final speech in the play. That speech, which commends the virtues of wifely obedience to a husband's honest will, is often seen as being appallingly sycophantic. Taken at face value, it does appear to be overly submissive, but couldn't it instead be a mischievous practical joke played on the two women to whom Kate addresses her comments, and whom she does not like? Indeed, there is support in the play itself for this interpretation. In addition, I did not find evidence in my Tarot reading for a broken and subjugated Kate.

After doing this reading, I thought it might be interesting to see if I could use cards 2 and 3 (which discuss Petruchio and Kate) to find the astrological signs of these two characters by using charts that associate birthdays with the various Tarot cards. Skipping the details of this investigation, the following is what I discovered.

For Petruchio, the Five of Pentacles implies that his birthday lies between April 21 and April 30. This shows him to be a Taurus, which makes sense as it implies that he is patient, possessive, and practical. Kate's Knight of Wands places her birthday between July 12 and August 11, which makes her sign either Cancer or Leo. From the evidence of the play, though, she is much more likely to be a Leo, which also makes perfect sense. I will leave it to those who have an interest in astrology to draw their own conclusions about these two characters and their interactions based on the above guesses about their astrological signs. However, based on this evidence, it does seem that they were not destined to have an easy time together.

Specific Notes About Individual Positions in the Spread

POSITION ONE: WHAT IS THE DIVINE WILL IN THIS RELATIONSHIP?

The card in this first position may explore the spiritual meaning that lies behind baffling or troublesome issues in the querent's relationship, or it may be concerned with the spiritual lessons that she needs to learn from those problems. In either case, the problem with interpreting this card often seems to lie in the identification of what is spiritual and what is not. Every lesson can have both a mundane and a divine aspect, with the difference between the two being rather subjective. Certainly, the physical self can be a vehicle for our soulful expression, and our spiritual growth brings meaning to our material world. So when we interpret the first card in this spread, we should try not to worry too much about whether or not the message appears to be sufficiently "spiritual," since even seemingly mundane lessons can be a vehicle for spiritual development and enlightenment.

POSITION TWO: HOW CAN YOU FIND APPRECIATION FOR THE BEST ATTRIBUTES OF YOUR HUSBAND?

Often when there are problems in our relationships, we are tempted to focus on the shortcomings of the other person and to place blame there. The second position in this spread is designed to find the beauty and goodness within the other person in order to facilitate the healing of the relationship. Admittedly, when a somewhat problematic card comes up here, this can be hard to do, but with a little care and patience, the message will come through. For example, it was hard at first to find virtue in the Five of Pentacles until I remembered that an old, traditional meaning for this card was that of a lover or a marriage. In light of that, we can see the two miserable souls in this card as having stuck together "for better or for worse." Also, the glaring wretchedness of these figures often distracts our attention from the beauty of the stained-glass window behind them, but it is there that we find the five pentacles that define this card, and it was there that I saw the place of peace and beauty that Kate could find through an appreciation for her husband.

POSITION THREE: HOW CAN YOU EXPRESS YOURSELF IN THIS RELATIONSHIP?

We often have too little understanding of how we express ourselves in our relationships. We can be sarcastic, belligerent, stubborn, overbearing, sullen, or submissive and not realize it. While it is crucial to identify our inappropriate modes of self-expression in order to improve our relationships, finding positive and suitable ways to express ourselves is just as important. Consequently, rather than being an accusation of the querent's failings, the card in position 3 should help her find better ways of expressing herself in her relationship.

In Kate's reading, the reversed Knight of Wands was perhaps the most fitting card that could have come up in this position. Nevertheless, it would have been easy to look at it and say, "Hey, this card says that you're way too brash, impulsive, and headstrong. Knock it off." That hardly seemed supportive, encouraging, or empowering though, so I opted for the more constructive comments that were used in this reading.

POSITION FOUR: HOW CAN YOU FIND PEACE IN THIS RELATIONSHIP?

This position is the first of several that address specific facets of the querent's relationship. This one is about peace, while cards 5, 6, and 9 are about playfulness, passion, and delight (respectively). Each of these aspects is important to the health and welfare of a relationship, and the card that comes up in each position can help the querent manifest or nurture that aspect, warn her of obstacles that may be blocking it, or suggest that it may be very hard to find that quality in her relationship. However, even if one of these cards seems problematic, I try not to give up easily on the indicated quality, since each card can give some sort of advice and encouragement.

POSITION FIVE: WHERE CAN YOU FIND PLAYFULNESS IN THIS RELATIONSHIP?

Playfulness is another important part of a relationship, and position five tries to help the querent find it. Of the four characteristics of a relationship that this spread deals with (peace, playfulness, passion, and delight), playfulness may seem the least important. However, we should not skim over card 5, making the erroneous assumption that its message is relatively insignificant. Without a sense of play, a relationship can quickly become staid, boring, and routine. Playfulness is as important as passion in keeping a relationship vibrantly alive, and the card in this position can help the querent discover (or rediscover) this valuable characteristic.

POSITION SIX: HOW CAN YOU IGNITE THE ARDOR AND PASSION IN THIS RELATIONSHIP?

Passion in a relationship is like the hearth in a premodern home. The embers can fade to a dull glow without endangering those who live in the house, but if the hearth goes completely cold, soon life in the home will too. Of course, a loss of passion is not the problem in every troubled relationship, and when it is not, this card may instead show the querent how the passion in her relationship can help heal it. However, even when the passion has died down, rekindling the fire is not an insurmountable problem as long as there is a spark left, and card 6 can help the querent see how to do that.

What happens, though, if a card comes up here that seems to be anything *but* passionate? In Kate's reading, the Nine of Wands initially seemed to be more discouraging than helpful. However, this is an example of where a little contemplation about a card may lead to advice or wisdom that may help the querent. In this case, although the Nine of Wands warned that the querent's defensiveness might be turning her passion into a barrier, it also suggested how she might express her passion better.

Finally, it is worth noting that although card 6 refers to passion and ardor, this does not necessarily have a sexual connotation. The passion that it refers to may be the strong feelings that two people have for each other or the excitement and enthusiasm that they have for being together.

POSITION SEVEN: HOW CAN YOU SEE THIS RELATIONSHIP MORE CLEARLY?

There are a couple of ways to interpret the intent of this position. First, it may help the querent understand her relationship better by giving her insights into it or explanations of what is going on in it. On the other hand, it may provide advice as to how the querent can find her own understanding of her relationship. It may also do both. In any case, our intuition and experience will help us decide which way to use the card that comes up in this position.

POSITION EIGHT: HOW CAN YOU BOTH BRING THE DIVINE INTO THIS RELATIONSHIP?

This card returns us to the concept of the role of the divine in the querent's relationship. We began with a consideration of divine will in the first position, and now after having examined the querent's relationship from various perspectives in cards 2 through 7, we can look at how we may endow it with divine essence. What does this mean? Although the intent of this position is not always easy to understand, we can find some clues if we refer back to its source.

The figure on the *World Spirit Tarot* Lovers card that inspired this position is a cherub standing in the typical Magician pose with one hand pointing upward and one hand pointing down. It depicts someone who is a conduit for drawing down spiritual energy. It says that our earthly being is a manifestation of our spirituality, and it is our spirituality that imbues our lives with meaning. With that in mind, we see that the card in this position can reveal how to put a sense of soulfulness back into the querent's relationship. This can revitalize her relationship, and it can help her find deeper meaning in it. Ultimately, however, finding and realizing the spiritual aspects of a relationship depends on both partners. The querent only can control her own actions, of course, but this card may comment on her partner's willingness to bring a spiritual dimension into their relationship as well.

Finally, this position and the first one, when considered together, can reveal the spiritual depth of the reading. Thus they provide a context in which to interpret the more down-to-earth meanings of the other cards in this spread. In Kate's reading, it is remarkable that the Hanged Man and the Empress came up in these two positions since both cards are about love: the unselfish love of the Hanged Man and the marital (or motherly) love of the Empress. This, more than anything else in this reading, was strong encouragement for the eventual success of Kate's marriage, and it influenced the course of the entire reading.

Position Nine: What Is the Delight in This Relationship?

The last position in this spread can be harder to figure out than some of the others since the concept of delight may be subtler than peace, playfulness, or passion. However, its ambiguity opens up the range of possibilities for the card that is dealt here. This card can remind the querent of the joy and happiness that this relationship can bring her, it can suggest how she might find more pleasure and enjoyment there, or it can discuss how this relationship might satisfy her wants and needs.

On the other hand, the comment of the ninth card may be a warning about the querent's delight in her relationship. In Kate's reading, the Devil card provided encouragement and advice, but it seemed to insist on providing a warning as well. A common interpretation of the Devil card involves our addictions to our desires, and the image on the Robin Wood version depicts two people caught in a trap. As a consequence of these considerations, I saw a warning here (supported by the messages of other cards in this reading) that Kate's passionate nature, if uncontrolled, could turn the potential delight of her marriage into a trap.

Other Notes About This Spread

The larger the spread, the more complex the interrelationships between the cards. In a spread like the Lovers Card spread, which has nine positions, these interrelationships provide a significant source of meaning. For example, this section's reading began with some general observations based on the number of major arcana cards, reversed cards, and cards from the four suits. Of course, it is valuable to start a reading with such insights no matter what the spread, but it is even more important with larger spreads. This is because the overview provided by such general observations lends a unified message, tone, or theme that can encapsulate a reading that may turn out to be complicated due to its large number of cards. In addition, such observations may influence the subsequent interpretations of the individual cards as well as the final conclusions about the reading. However, while a preliminary overview gives us a first impression about a reading, it is not the final word on the subject.

Besides gaining overall impressions from all of the cards, we also can find additional meaning in smaller groupings of cards in the spread. Most large spreads contain clusters of cards that can be considered subsidiary spreads or subspreads, and we can do quick minireadings using them. This practice often leads to greater insights about the individual cards by putting them in a context that is of a manageable size (typically two to four cards), and it provides additional messages via the interpretations of these subspreads. The following are subspreads embedded in the Lovers Card spread that I like to use. You, however, may find different ones that better suit your understanding of this spread or that more closely serve your particular needs.

First, there is the general relationship subspread, composed of cards 6, 2, 3, and 7. This line of cards shows the querent and her partner within the context of their relationship and its passion. Of course, embedded within this subspread is another important cluster, which focuses on the querent and her partner: cards 2 and 3.

Next, cards 1, 8, and 9 focus on divinity in the relationship. I included card 9 here because I consider delight to be both an expression of the divine and its gift. Alternatively, we might focus on just cards 1 and 8, which explicitly relate the divine to the querent's relationship.

Finally, I sometimes like to use the two-card subspread composed of cards 4 and 6 (peace and passion) in order to examine the contrast between these two disparate characteristics, and cards 5 and 6 (playfulness and passion) for their comparison of two similar, yet distinct, characteristics.

Alternative Spreads

An easy way to create your own personalized version of this section's spread is to reinterpret the symbols on the *World Spirit Tarot's* Lovers card for yourself. For example, if you see lilies as purity (instead of clarity), you might change position seven to be something like, "How can you purify your attitudes about this relationship?" Or considering that Kuan Yin is the Chinese goddess of mercy and a personification of compassion, you could redefine position four to be about exhibiting mercy or compassion in the relationship.

Similarly, I have redefined the Lovers Card spread in order to create a version of it that is suitable for "looking for love" questions. The result is the following set of positional meanings, which can be attributed to the same layout that is illustrated at the beginning of this section in Figure 18.

1. What kind of a relationship is your spiritual purpose guiding you toward?

2. What kind of person would be best for you?

3. What can you do to prepare yourself for a loving relationship?

4. How can you find peace and serenity as you search for a relationship?

5. How can humor and a light heart help you find a relationship?

6. How do your passions define what you need in a relationship?

7. How might you purify your relationship needs?

8. How can you manifest your spiritual purpose in a relationship?

9. What delights you most in a relationship?

Other Tarot cards may serve as inspiration for a spread as well. For example, another relationship spread may be created based on the more traditional Lovers card image, as designed by A. E. Waite: the angel above, the woman and man in the foreground, the serpent in the tree of knowledge behind the woman, the flaming tree of life behind the man, and the mountain between the two people. In that case, the elements of that card may inspire a spread like the one in Figure 19.

These cards may be interpreted using the following positional meanings:

1. What is the guidance for this relationship from your higher self?

2. How does your partner see you in this relationship?

3. What do you want or need from this relationship?

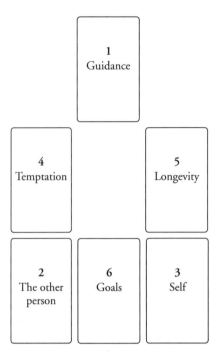

Figure 19. The Waite Lovers Card spread.

4. What temptation do you face or do you need to resist?

5. What can help you make this relationship last?

6. What goals or aspirations do the two of you share in this relationship?

Similarly, other cards that might serve as inspiration for a spread include the Chariot for a spread about achieving success, Justice for one that focuses on how to gain a fairer or more balanced understanding of a situation, or the Sun for finding joy or enlightenment.[19] However, inspiration need not be limited to Tarot cards. Any image that grabs your attention, piques your interest, or sparks your imagination—from classical works of art to commercial ads in magazines—may lead you to create a new Tarot spread. The world is filled with images, each one replete with symbols, and each one with its own Tarot spread just waiting to be discovered.

---

19. For a detailed description of a Hanged Man spread, see Mary K. Greer's *The Complete Book of Tarot Reversals* (220–22).

THE MODIFIED CELTIC CROSS RELATIONSHIP SPREAD

A Six-Card Spread

The ten-card Celtic Cross spread is perhaps the best known and most commonly used Tarot spread. It is described in many beginning Tarot books, taught by many Tarot teachers, and used by many Tarot readers. There is good reason for its popularity: it is elegant in its design, general in its applicability, and complex in the depth of information it affords. However, its complexity and general applicability can make it unsuitable for some purposes.

For example, for a brief period a few years ago I did Tarot readings over the telephone. Since a large percentage of my calls were about relationships, I wanted to use a spread specifically focused on that subject. Also, using all ten cards of the Celtic Cross was much too time consuming for telephone readings. At the same time, I wanted to create a spread that retained some of the elegance and depth of the Celtic Cross, so I decided to keep the six cards of the major cross (cards 1 through 6) but eliminate the four-card "staff" that makes up the right side of that spread (cards 7 through 10) (see Figure 22 on page 135). I then reworded the positional meanings of the six cards that remained, preserving the basic themes of the original positions while focusing their attention on issues concerning relationships.

It is important to note that although my original intention was to create a spread to deal with romantic relationships, the result is one that can be applied to relationships of any type—platonic as well as romantic—and in any situation where a moderately sized reading is appropriate.

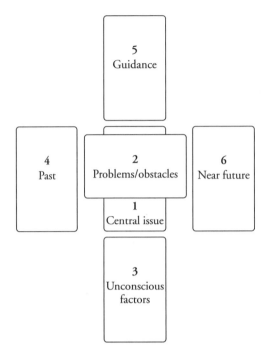

Figure 20. The Modified Celtic Cross Relationship spread.

The Spread

Lay out six cards as in Figure 20.

Interpret these cards using positional meanings based on the following suggestions:

1. **Central issue.** What do you want out of this relationship? What personal issues are you dealing with in this relationship?

2. **Problems/obstacles.** What is blocking your desire? What is the basic problem in this relationship? (*Note that this card is laid sideways, crossing the first card.*)

3. **Unconscious factors.** What underlying or unseen influences are at work in your relationship? What unconscious aspects of your personality are affecting this relationship?

4. **Past.** What do you need to know about the background or history of this relationship? What events or influences from your past are affecting your participation in this relationship?

5. **Guidance of your higher self.** What can help you? What can you do to help yourself? What spiritual purpose does this relationship fulfill?

6. **Near future.** Where is this relationship headed? What is the probable outcome of this relationship?

I have provided more than one question for each card position. You may choose one of them or use a combination or synthesis of them. Of course, you should make this choice before dealing the cards, as I have done for the following reading.

A KnightHawk Reading with the Modified Celtic Cross Relationship Spread

Dear KnightHawk,

I am very concerned about my friend, Dorian Gray. He is an innocent young man of extraordinary personal beauty who has inspired me to create the best painting of my career: his portrait. The problem is that Dorian has recently met another friend of mine, Lord Henry, who I fear is a very bad influence on the boy. Already I can see how Lord Henry manipulates and corrupts him. But Dorian seems to have taken a fancy to Lord Henry, and so I fear that Lord Henry will take away from me this person who greatly inspires me as an artist.

What can I do to save my friendship with Dorian? And how can I protect him from the corrosive influence of Lord Henry?

Most sincerely yours,
Basil Hallward

*   *   *

Dear Mr. Hallward,

Thank you for requesting this Tarot reading. You have posed a couple of questions here, so please allow me to rephrase them into one question that can be addressed effectively by a Tarot reading: what do you need to know or do in order to maintain a satisfying friendship with Dorian Gray that will serve the best interests of both of you?

The cards that I have dealt for this question are as follows:

1. What do you want out of this relationship?
   King of Swords reversed

2. What is the basic problem in this relationship?
   Eight of Cups

3. What underlying or unseen influences are at work in your relationship?
   Queen of Pentacles reversed

4. What do you need to know about the background or history of this relationship?
   Four of Cups

5. What can help you, or what can you do to help yourself?
   The Hermit reversed

6. What is the probable outcome of this relationship?
   Three of Swords reversed

First, the King of Swords indicates a need to be an authority figure—perhaps even a father figure—to this young man. Since this card is reversed, however, I see that you have not realized or acknowledged this desire, and in addition, it is a difficult role for you to play. Similarly, I see here a subliminal need to control this relationship, although your intentions are benign, even generous.

The problem in this relationship, as evidenced by the Eight of Cups, is that you give up too easily on your true feelings, and you have denied or turned your back on your emotional investment in this relationship. You have indicated that Lord Henry's influence on Dorian is waxing, while you fear yours is waning. Might this be due to you not facing your emotional attachment to your friendship with Dorian? Perhaps, like the King of Swords, you strive to maintain an emotional distance, keeping your interactions with Dorian on a purely intellectual basis. In this case, the Eight of Cups says that this detachment is part of the problem. Like the figure in that card, both you and Dorian are too willing to walk away from this friendship because you both fail to recognize or acknowledge the significance of its emotional content.

The next card, the Queen of Pentacles, is notable in that its depiction of a nurturing mother is an interesting contrast to the stern father figure of the King of Swords. Since this card is reversed, it implies that Dorian has an unmet need to be nurtured, and this need influences the course of his relationships. Thus, it urges you to be less of an authoritative father figure (like the King of Swords) and more nurturing to him, although this card's reversed aspect indicates how hard that can be for you.

The Four of Cups suggests an air of ennui, and it expands upon the message of the Eight of Cups. It says that Dorian has become dissatisfied with his friendship with you. It is not that there is strife or conflict in it, but rather that he has found it lacking an emotional foundation, and thus he has become bored with it. Also, in this card there is a shining new cup being offered, which indicates that Dorian has come to see Lord Henry as that exciting new element in his life. This is in contrast to the repressed emotions of your relationship with him.

The advice of the reversed Hermit is to stop trying so hard to be a mentor to your young friend. It seems that Dorian resists that sort of an approach, and it is straining your relationship with him. In addition, this card urges you to search inside yourself for answers and fulfillment, which it also says you have avoided doing. Perhaps, as we saw with the Eight of Cups, it is the emotional content of your relationship with Dorian that you resist exploring, but that you need to understand. On a more mundane (and literal) level, the reversed Hermit card may be urging you to get out more. Be less of a hermit yourself, and maybe then you will depend less upon this one particular friendship.

I am afraid the last card, the reversed Three of Swords, does not bode well for this relationship. If you continue as you have, all of your advice to Dorian—however well intentioned it may be—might eventually lead to pain and sorrow, as he continues to see it as hurtful interference. This card also warns that Dorian may become cold, heartless, and unfeeling. However, since this card is reversed, these results will be long in coming, so you have time to change your approach, if you can, and thus, to change the possible future that this card indicates.

Now let me examine one particular cluster of cards within this spread: cards 4, 1, and 6, which may be seen as a Past, Present, Future spread. Considered together, these three cards tell a story that emphasizes what I have said previously. They say that one or both of you has become unhappy with the emotional content of this relationship. Rather than deepen its emotional aspects, you tend to advise and lecture Dorian, which makes you more like an authority figure than a friend. This is something that Dorian neither wants nor needs at this time, so this approach will slowly turn him away from you. In fact, although it will take a while, it is an approach that may result in painful arguments and even a wounding of your relationship.

In summary, these cards say that Dorian deeply needs love, compassion, and nurturing, not instruction, criticism, and advice about how to live his life. The guidance of this reading, then, is to face the emotional aspects of this friendship, and to get in touch with your feelings about it.

Thank you for requesting this reading, Mr. Hallward. I hope it helps you.

Best of luck,
KnightHawk

Comments on a Reading with the Modified Celtic Cross Relationship Spread

For the sake of those who have not read Oscar Wilde's *The Picture of Dorian Gray,* the following is a brief synopsis of the story.

Basil Hallward has painted a portrait of his handsome young friend, Dorian Gray, who is envious of the fact that the painting's beauty will last forever. Dorian wishes that it would age instead of him, so that he might remain eternally youthful while it takes on "the lines of suffering and thought," and amazingly, he gets his wish.

Apparently free from having to pay the wages of sin, Dorian begins to lead a dissolute life. Little by little the portrait, now hidden in Dorian's attic, shows evidence of his descent into debauchery while he himself does not. Thus he retains a look of youth and innocence, even as he becomes increasingly worldly, self-absorbed, and cruel. Years later, when Basil finally sees what has become of the portrait after years of Dorian's decadent living, he urges his friend to repent his sins. In response, Dorian, now completely corrupted, kills his old friend in a fit of rage.[20]

Although Dorian's body is immune to the effects of his degradation, his soul is not. He spirals into despair and self-loathing, until finally, at the end of the story, he stabs his portrait, the record and horrible reminder of what he has done with his life. As a result, he dies, transformed into the hideous thing he has become, while the picture reverts to its original beauty.

Often I learn something new about the querent when I do these KnightHawk readings, but in this case, the greatest insight I got was into the character of Oscar Wilde himself. Many critics have said that the clever and acerbic Lord Henry is a reflection of Wilde, and certainly many of his lines could have issued from Wilde's own lips. However, as I did this reading, I saw, via the King of Swords, that Wilde put much of himself into Basil Hallward as well, since Wilde, like Hallward, often tried to be an authority figure to young men in his own life. Indeed, modeling the doomed Basil Hallward after a part of himself was sadly prophetic, for one of Wilde's attempts at being an authority figure contributed significantly to his tragic fate. Considered in this light, I saw past the commonly held image of a witty and urbane Oscar Wilde, and I was able to catch a glimpse of the vulnerable and lonely Basil Hallward within him. (Some months after writing this, I found the following quote from Oscar Wilde: "Basil Hallward is what I think I am; Lord Henry what the world thinks of me; Dorian what I would like to be—in other ages, perhaps."[21])

Specific Notes About Individual Positions in the Spread

POSITION ONE: WHAT DO YOU WANT OUT OF THIS RELATIONSHIP?
This position lies at the heart of the Modified Celtic Cross Relationship spread, and the card that comes up here is pivotal to a reading with this spread. It sets the tone for the whole reading, and its meaning influences the interpretations of the other cards. This was

---

20. It is an eerie coincidence that Dorian stabbed Basil Hallward, considering that the Three of Swords turned up in the "Probable outcome" position in this section's reading.

21. Oscar Wilde, *The Picture of Dorian Gray* (New York: Random House, Modern Library, 1998), back cover.

particularly true in this section's reading wherein the reversed King of Swords, with its cold, authoritative, and emotionally detached air, was a pervasive influence throughout the rest of the reading.

When card 1's message is unexpected, its persistent impact can make a reading with this spread hard for a querent to accept. Although most querents assume that they know what they want in a relationship, sometimes they are taken aback by the message of this card, and as a result they might deny its validity. For example, in the reading for Basil Hallward, card 1 was a reversed court card. This indicated that unconscious or repressed motives and personality traits were at work (which are common causes of denial) and so Hallward probably would have found the message of this card, and of the entire reading, difficult to accept.

POSITION TWO: WHAT IS THE BASIC PROBLEM IN THIS RELATIONSHIP?
The card in this position is unusual in that it is laid at a right angle to the other cards, on top of and crossing the first card. This makes its orientation (reversed or not) ambiguous, so I ignore reversals for this one card. Instead, considering the meaning of this position, I always look for the problematic aspects of this card. In this reading, the Eight of Cups came up here, and this card is one that I find to be rather balanced (i.e., neither especially "good" nor "bad"). So it was not hard to find its problematic aspects, especially when viewed in light of the card it was crossing: the King of Swords.

This brings up another point about this position. The cards in the first two positions are closely related, lying at the heart of this spread (as they also lie at the heart of the full Celtic Cross), so each should be viewed in light of the other.[22] Thus, the problematic aspects seen in this second card should be related back to the issue that was brought up by the first card. For example, in this reading, I directly related the reversed King of Swords's emotional distance and purely intellectual way of relating to other people to the message in the Eight of Cups concerning the rejection of an emotional investment.

POSITION THREE: WHAT UNDERLYING OR UNSEEN INFLUENCES ARE AT WORK IN YOUR RELATIONSHIP?
While doing these KnightHawk readings, I often find that some cards fit their situation amazingly well, and in this section's reading, the meaning of the reversed Queen of Pen-

---

22. There is an entire book that concentrates on just this minispread: *The Heart of the Tarot* by Sandra A. Thomson, Robert E. Mueller, and Signe E. Echols.

tacles was remarkably clear. This Queen often represents a generous and nurturing mother, which was significant considering the fate of Dorian's mother. Lady Margaret Devereux had married a poor soldier, which displeased her aristocratic father to such a great extent that he engineered the death of the unfortunate young man. Devastated by this loss, Lady Margaret, who had been pregnant at the time of her husband's death, died not long after giving birth to Dorian. The resulting lack of a loving and caring mother must have been crucial to the development of Dorian's character, leaving him with an aching need for a nurturing mother, which affected all of his subsequent relationships.

Note that this position (underlying or unseen influences) is one where people usually expect to find the unexpected, as opposed to position one, where the querent typically assumes that he will see a card with an unsurprising message. In this reading, Basil Hallward may have known that Dorian lost his mother at an early age, but he probably failed to realize how profoundly that loss affected the youth and his relationships. Thus, the critical influence of her death on the development of his friendship with Dorian would have seemed both underlying and unseen from Hallward's point of view.

POSITION FOUR: WHAT DO YOU NEED TO KNOW ABOUT THE BACKGROUND OR HISTORY OF THIS RELATIONSHIP?

This position could be labeled simply "The past," and in fact its corresponding position in the ten-card Celtic Cross spread generally is called exactly that. However, in creating this spread, I renamed it because "The past" seemed too vague for the specific intent of a relationship reading. In a reading with this spread, the fourth card is intended to focus on the past as it pertains specifically to the relationship in question. For example, the Four of Cups could have referred to a general feeling of ennui, perhaps in Dorian's life or maybe in Basil's. However, such a general interpretation would not have been as helpful as the one given, which was related specifically to their friendship.

POSITION FIVE: WHAT CAN HELP YOU, OR WHAT CAN YOU DO TO HELP YOURSELF?

Sometimes the card in this position indicates something or someone in the querent's life that can help him with his problem. In that case, the better portion of its advice is that the querent should avail himself of that assistance. However, in many readings (including the one in this section), the card in the fifth position contains advice as to what the querent can do to help himself. In fact, in this reading, the reversed Hermit gave Basil Hallward several pieces of advice for resolving his problems with his friendship with Dorian.

POSITION SIX: WHAT IS THE PROBABLE OUTCOME OF THIS RELATIONSHIP?

The "Probable outcome" card is not a set-in-stone declaration of what the future will be, but an indication of where this relationship is headed if things keep going the way they are. Of course, this outcome can be affected by the querent (or by other people in his life), and I try to stress this fact when I talk about the meaning of this card. Thus, in this reading I used phrases like, "If you continue as you have . . ." and ". . . you have time to change your approach." Also, this way of interpreting the card in this position means that it will offer, at least implicitly, some valuable advice for the querent.

Other Notes About This Spread

As noted in the previous section, we can gain additional understanding of a reading when we work with subsidiary spreads embedded within the main spread. In the Modified Celtic Cross Relationship spread (as in the larger Celtic Cross itself), an obvious sub-spread is the three-card Past, Present, Future spread indicated by cards 4, 1, and 6. The implications of this cluster of cards were explored in this section's reading, but other sub-spreads can be considered as well. For example, we might interpret cards 1, 2, and 5 as a three-card Situation, Problem, Advice spread.

Another way of synthesizing an integrated whole out of the individual cards is to summarize the major themes that have expressed themselves in the course of the reading. Is there a basic observation, warning, or piece of advice repeatedly stated or implied by the cards? Is there a pervasive tone underlying the messages of the cards? After making sense of the cards, both individually and in small clusters, I try to find an overall summary for a reading. In this section's reading, I saw that the contrast between Dorian's emotional needs and Basil Hallward's intellectual approach to their friendship was a repeated theme, and it seemed to be this reading's most important point. Thus, this consideration led to the summarization that concluded this reading.

Alternative Spreads

For some of the spreads introduced in this book, I have shown how a new spread can be developed by expanding an old one. This section demonstrates the opposite: a new spread was developed by reducing an old one, thereby narrowing its focus. Taking this process even further, we could use cards 1, 2, 5, and 6 from the Modified Celtic Cross Relationship spread to create the spread in Figure 21.

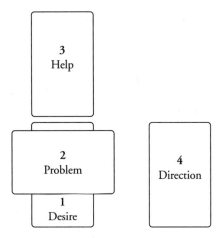

Figure 21. The Abbreviated Celtic Cross Relationship spread.

These cards may be interpreted as follows:

1. What do you want out of this relationship?

2. What is the basic problem in this relationship?

3. What can help you improve this relationship?

4. Where is it headed?

Alternatively, we can create a more generalized version of this section's spread by removing its focus on relationships in order to create a new spread that would be applicable to almost any situation. It would use the same card layout as the Modified Celtic Cross Relationship spread, but the positional definitions would be phrased more generally. For example, we could use the following positional meanings:

1. What is the most important issue you are dealing with at this time in your life?

2. What are the problems or obstacles you face regarding this issue?

3. What underlying or unseen influences are at work in your situation?

4. What events from your past are influencing you right now?

5. What can help you overcome the problems or obstacles you face?

6. What is the probable outcome of your situation?

Finally, the most obvious alternative spread is the ten-card Celtic Cross spread itself.[23] This common spread is described in many sources, including many of the little white books that often accompany Tarot decks, although every source provides its own unique take on how to use it. The Celtic Cross layout that I use is shown in Figure 22, and what follows is a description of how I interpret its card positions.

1. **The central issue of the reading.** This card describes or comments on the basic issue of the reading, thus providing a focus for it. If a general reading has been requested (i.e., if no specific question has been posed), this card can define what the main issue is. Even when a question has been asked, however, this card might define which aspects of that question are important to consider, or it may redefine the question in such a way that it redirects the course of the reading.

2. **Problems or obstacles.** Card 2 shows the conflict, obstacle, or antagonist that is causing problems within the context of the central issue.

3. **Unconscious factors.** This card deals with issues relevant to the reading that lie within the unconscious mind of the querent or about which he is unaware. Another common meaning for this position is "Foundation," in which case, it describes what forms the basis of the current situation.

4. **The past.** In reflecting the querent's past, card 4 may indicate factors that are diminishing in the querent's life or that he needs to release. In general, though, the understanding of past events that this card brings can help put current events into a meaningful context.

5. **Conscious factors.** This card comments on the querent's beliefs, preconceived notions, and attitudes regarding the issues of this reading. Consequently, it may lead the querent to see another point of view, or it may reinforce his beliefs. Another common meaning for this position is "Higher consciousness," which may be interpreted to mean advice from the querent's higher self.

---

23. A sample KnightHawk Tarot reading with the Celtic Cross spread appears in my book *Tarot Tells the Tale*.

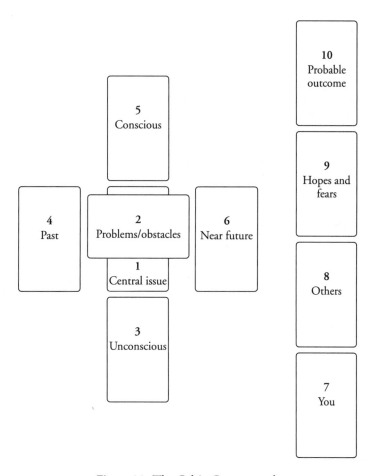

Figure 22. The Celtic Cross spread.

6. **The future.** This card depicts the probable near future—that is, where the querent's life is headed if things keep going the way they are now. Sometimes this card advises the querent as to the next step he needs to take to overcome the obstacles depicted in the second card.

7. **The querent.** This card discusses things about the querent that affect his situation and the central issue of the reading. These things can span the spectrum from strengths to weaknesses.

8. **The querent's environment.** This card talks about relevant issues, people, conditions, or events in the world around the querent, how they are affecting the central issue of the reading, and whether they are helping or hindering the querent.

9. **Hopes and fears.** This card depicts the querent's expectations—either good (hopes) or bad (fears)—and sometimes it recommends how to act upon them or cope with them. Often hopes and fears are closely related, being opposing sides of the same coin.

10. **Probable outcome.** This card examines how the querent's situation probably will end up given the influences at work now and how the querent is dealing with them.

In addition to interpreting the individual cards in this spread, it is valuable to consider some of the subordinate spreads embedded within it. The following are a few suggested subspreads that can be used.

- Cards 4, 1, and 6 form a three-card Past, Present, Future spread.

- Cards 3, 1, and 5 address different levels of consciousness about the querent's situation: what he is not aware of, what is really going on, and what he thinks is happening.

- Cards 1 and 2, sometimes called "the minicross," may be read as a two-card Background, Problem spread.

- Cards 1, 2, 9, and 10 define a Background, Problem, Advice, and Probable Outcome spread when we consider that hopes and fears (card 9) hold the seeds of advice that can carry the querent to the probable outcome.

- Cards 7 and 8 form a dualistic spread that covers the querent and his environment (i.e., his inner reality and outer reality).

There are many other ways to cluster some of the cards in the Celtic Cross, so your intuition may reveal other subspreads that can lead you to a deeper understanding of a reading with this spread.

THE NEW YEAR'S RESOLUTION SPREAD
A Six-Card Spread

At the 2002 San Francisco Bay Area Tarot Symposium I presented a workshop on creating spreads. Afterward, one of the participants asked me if I could suggest a spread she might use to do a birthday reading for her sister. She told me that she had done these birthday readings for several years now, but this year she was inspired by my workshop to create a spread that would be specifically tailored for the occasion and for her sister. I asked her to tell me a little bit about her sister. The detail that stood out the most was the fact that this woman's sister was a cook, so I suggested that she create a spread with positions based on the ingredients of a birthday cake. For example, sugar might suggest what is sweet in her life; flour, the main ingredient of the coming year; eggs, new beginnings that she is facing; milk, what nurtures her; and candles, her wishes for the coming year.

That conversation reminded me that sometimes we are called upon to do readings on holidays or special occasions such as birthdays, weddings, anniversaries, Halloween, Thanksgiving, or New Year's Day. Of course we can use a general, tried-and-true spread at such times, but wouldn't a distinctive spread designed specifically for such an occasion facilitate a reading that is more meaningful and festive? With that in mind, I created the New Year's Resolution spread that is illustrated in this section, and on the following New Year's Eve I used it for a Tarot reading that proved to be very effective.

To create this spread, I first considered that one of the unique things about our celebration of the new year is the fact that we make New Year's resolutions. The choice and formation of a resolution is not always easy, however, so I decided to let the wisdom of the Tarot suggest one with the first card in the spread, which I put in the center since it would be pivotal to the reading.

Next, I thought about various characteristics of New Year's resolutions, which led me to create the remaining spread positions. First of all, since we tend to react to our resolutions with both hopes and fears, I placed a card for hopes above the central card and one for fears below it, an ordering that reflects how I conceptualize these two reactions. I also realized that sometimes the reasons for our resolutions are mysterious, even to us. Resolutions may arise out of a desire for gain, a need for atonement, a wish to break a bad habit or to create a good one, or a yearning for self-improvement, but we may not know which of these reasons have impelled us. Since I was asking the Tarot to propose the resolution, I decided to let it also indicate the reason behind it. Consequently, I placed a card to that effect behind the central card.

In my first pass at this spread, I completed it with a card to indicate the probable outcome if we keep this resolution. However, as I thought about the resulting spread, it struck me that another important aspect of our New Year's resolutions is the fact that we so often break them in a disconcertingly short amount of time. Consequently, I added a card that could warn of obstacles that might interfere with keeping this resolution, thereby preparing us to deal with such problems before they arise. I placed this obstacle card between the resolution card and the probable outcome card, since that is where it lies in our lives.

The result, then, is a spread that suggests a New Year's resolution, that explores its meaning, and that prepares us to keep it. Of course, we do not always need a Tarot reading to come up with a good New Year's resolution. If we already have one in mind, we can change the definition of the first position to be "What do you need to know about your New Year's resolution?" In either case, the New Year's Resolution spread can shed valuable light on whatever resolution you decide to use.

The most obvious time to use this spread is either on New Year's Eve (in which case it can be a positive alternative to the popular ritual of drinking too much) or on New Year's Day. However, this spread can be useful at the beginning of any new cycle (not just at the new calendar year) by substituting the word "commitment" for "New Year's resolution." Thus, for example, we can use it for birthday readings to reinvigorate our life or for anniversary readings to reaffirm our commitment in a relationship.

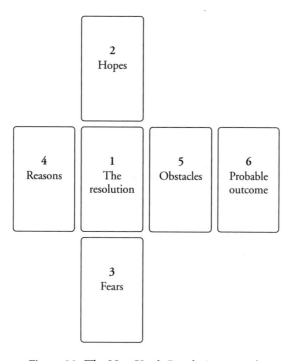

Figure 23. The New Year's Resolution spread.

The Spread

Begin by dealing six cards as indicated in Figure 23.

Interpret these cards using the following positional meanings:

1. What New Year's resolution might you make?

2. What are your hopes for it?

3. What are your fears about it?

4. Why should you make this resolution?

5. What obstacles may block you from keeping it?

6. What are the probable results of keeping this resolution?

A KnightHawk Reading with the New Year's Resolution Spread

Dear KnightHawk,

As the New Year approaches, my friends are urging me to make a New Year's resolution. Now, I know that some of them have problems that they need to resolve, but try as I might, I can't think of anything that I need to work on. Can the Tarot suggest a resolution that I should make for the coming year?

With warmest regards,
Don Juan

*   *   *

Dear Don Juan,

Thank you for this request. What follows is a reading to suggest a New Year's resolution for you. But it is more than just that. This reading also explains how this resolution can affect you and where it can lead you. The cards I have dealt for your reading are the following:

1. What New Year's resolution might you make?
   King of Cups

2. What are your hopes for it?
   King of Wands

3. What are your fears about it?
   Six of Swords

4. Why should you make this resolution?
   Five of Pentacles

5. What obstacles may block you from keeping it?
   Two of Cups reversed

6. What are the probable results of keeping this resolution?
   Six of Cups

The first card in this spread, the King of Cups, represents someone who is in control of his feelings, having reached a significant level of emotional maturity. He exhibits sympathy and compassion in his dealings with other people, and he has tempered the volatility of his feelings in order to reside in a state of tranquility, even when he finds himself in the midst of an emotionally turbulent situation. This suggests that your New Year's resolution could be to maintain more control over your emotions or to find ways to express them more maturely. Alternatively, since the suit of Cups also deals with relationships, you could make a resolution to find a mature and stable romantic relationship. Considering that in this spread this King faces the Two of Cups, which depicts a pair of committed lovers, my recommendation is that you use the final suggestion: to find a mature and stable romantic relationship. Of course, the choice is up to you.

The next two cards discuss your hopes and fears about your resolution. The King of Wands implies that your hopes may come from your pride and ego. It seems you hope that the maturation of your emotions and relationships will enhance your charismatic appeal and make you appear nobler and more like a leader in order to impress your peers. However, at a deeper level it may be saying that you hope to learn how to control your passions.

As for your fears, the Six of Swords indicates a concern that your resolution may take you through a difficult transition. The calm and somber shores toward which it can take you are disturbingly unfamiliar to you, since you are used to a much more exciting life. Also, your resolution may show you where you really belong and the person you are meant to be, and perhaps you fear that you won't like what you find. However, the unseen ferryman in this card indicates that a higher source is available to guide you along your journey should you decide to take it, and this soulful journey will lead you to a place in your life where you can find a truer sense of fulfillment than you have today.

A quick comparison, then, of these hopes and fears indicates that your primary concern about your New Year's resolution is how it will affect the level of excitement in your life. It seems, however, that it can take you to a higher plane where you can find a level of joy and satisfaction that transcends the thrills you are used to.

With the next card, the Five of Pentacles, we will examine some reasons for making your resolution. An obvious interpretation of this card is that it depicts loss and adversity, which could indicate misfortunes that you have caused others. In that case, this card says you need to be more mature in your relationships in order to stop causing such problems. On the other hand, this card could be a warning that hardships may befall you if you do not endeavor to make the self-improvements implicit in your New Year's resolution. For example, philandering may cause you to become a social outcast, a pariah. Looked at another way, this card can indicate that you have placed a high priority on physical comfort and material gain, but such prosperity can be quite fragile. Such an approach tends to result in a sort of poverty of the soul, which may be rectified by a commitment to achieving emotional maturity.

Next, the reversed Two of Cups indicates obstacles that might hinder your efforts to keep your New Year's resolution. On one level, the union of the man dressed in red and gold with the woman in blue and silver can represent a union of passion and spiritual love. Being reversed, however, this indicates that you have problems forging such a union within yourself, which can block the mature expression of your emotions and cripple your efforts to forge a mature relationship. The advice of this card, then, is to try to marry your passion to your feelings of love. For example, whenever passion arises, try to see if there is love there too. The reversed Two of Cups also may indicate resistance to making a loving commitment to another person and a propensity for having illicit love affairs instead. This, of course, will sabotage any truly meaningful relationships, so strive to keep your commitments and to avoid entering into brief, superficial affairs.

Finally, we come to the Six of Cups, which depicts the probable result of making and keeping your New Year's resolution. First of all, it is remarkable how much this card looks like an inverted reflection of the previous card. This assures you that you have the ability to overcome and resolve the problems indicated by the reversed Two of Cups. In addition, the Six of Cups signifies emotional innocence and sharing of love. At first glance, it may seem ironic that emotional maturity could lead to innocence. However, the emotional innocence indicated here is a rectification of the jaded attitude toward love and relationships that was implied by the reversed Two of Cups. It is the ability to share love unconditionally and with purity, as both children and mature lovers do. Most fundamentally, though, this card holds out the promise of a deep joy and sense of satisfaction that comes from giving unconditionally from the heart, and it shows the emotional support that you can get from others in return when you are able to do that.

In conclusion, this spread suggests that you make a New Year's resolution to find and maintain a mature romantic relationship this year. Although you may be concerned that this course will not be as exciting as your life has been so far, it will lead you to a richer and more fulfilling joy and to a prosperity of the soul, as well as insulate you from misfortunes that otherwise may be coming your way. However, it does require that you be determined to find love, not just passion, in your relationships.

Thank you for requesting this reading. I hope it helps you.

Best of luck,
KnightHawk

Comments on a Reading with the New Year's Resolution Spread

Early in the seventeenth century, a Spanish friar named Gabriel Téllez (using the pseudonym of Tirso de Molina) wrote a play called *El Burlador de Sevilla* (*The Trickster of Seville*) about a profligate lover and unrepentant seducer named Don Juan Tenorio. Since then, the legend of Don Juan has flourished, finding expression in a wide assortment of tales, including Lord Byron's masterpiece, *Don Juan*.[24]

---

24. There are, in fact, so many stories based on this popular figure that an entire bibliographic work is devoted to listing them. See Armand Singer, *A Bibliography of the Don Juan Theme* (Morgantown, WV: University of West Virginia Press, 1954).

At first I was tempted to use Byron's *Don Juan* as the basis for this section's reading due to the enduring power of that epic poem. Unfortunately, that Don Juan diverges significantly from the popular notion of this famous character in that, rather than being a womanizer and a libertine, Byron's hero tends to be an agreeable victim of a succession of ladies who cannot resist his charm and good looks. Realizing that this disparity could prove confusing, I decided against using that version, which left me with the question of which version of Don Juan to use for a reading.

I concluded that the best-known Don Juan is not the product of any one piece of literature. Instead, he is the legendary archetype that has arisen from a mixture of interpretations and has taken form in the collective imagination of our culture. This Don Juan is a scoundrel, a shameless liar, and an incorrigible lady-killer, but he is also a likable rogue in that he is cheerful and charismatic. This legendary figure, then, was the Don Juan for whom I did this section's reading.

Specific Notes About Individual Positions in the Spread

Position One: What New Year's Resolution Might You Make?

Discovering the resolution indicated by card 1 is usually the primary reason for doing a reading with the New Year's Resolution spread. Since this card is so essential, its message should be kept in mind during the rest of the reading in order to provide a focus for the interpretations of the other cards.

When working with this first card, there may be a temptation to tell the querent what resolution he should use. It is advisable, though, merely to suggest a resolution, or to provide several alternatives, in order to help the querent create his own. Although we can work with the querent in this process, the final decision should be his, since a resolution that he creates for himself will mean more to him than one he is given by someone else.

With that said, however, it is also important to note that we should encourage the querent to make a resolution that is as specific as reasonably possible. Initially, card 1 may suggest a general theme, but resolutions are more effective when they are specific. Otherwise, they are too easy to ignore, and it is too hard to evaluate how well we adhere to them. For example, once when I did a reading with this spread for a couple (see the alternative spread at the end of this section), the card that came up in position one was the Queen of Cups. The general theme that the couple saw in this card was that they should strive to strengthen and deepen their relationship. While this suggestion was relevant, it seemed too vague, so we worked together to come up with a two-part resolution. For them this was to spend Sunday evenings together, just the two of them, and to get away for a romantic weekend once every few months. This resolution was specific, productive, and measurable.

POSITIONS TWO AND THREE: WHAT ARE YOUR HOPES FOR IT? WHAT ARE YOUR FEARS ABOUT IT?

The hopes and fears indicated by the cards in positions two and three can lie at any level of the querent's consciousness. They may be at the forefront of his thoughts, or they may lurk in the shadowy depths of his unconscious mind. They may reside at some level between these extremes, or they may operate on several levels at once. For example, in this section's reading, the King of Wands said that Don Juan's hopes centered on what his resolution could do for him superficially, such as enhancing his charismatic appeal. It also implied that deep down, he really did want to be able to control his passions and become a better person.

In dealing with the querent's hopes and fears, it is relatively easy to discuss those that lie at the surface, but the ones buried deep inside are another matter. The querent may not recognize them, and sometimes he even may deny them strenuously. If so, all we can do is present what we see in the cards and let it go at that, trusting that the querent will cope with such information in his own time.

POSITION FOUR: WHY SHOULD YOU MAKE THIS RESOLUTION?

To find the reasons for this resolution, we should consider the card in position four in terms of the full spectrum of time, from the past to the future. For example, what events or circumstances from the querent's past might require rectitude or healing? What problems in the querent's present state of affairs need to be fixed? Is there a possible undesirable future development that a resolution might help the querent avoid? Examining questions like these can help the querent see why he should make this resolution, and in gaining such understanding, he may be further motivated to keep it.

POSITION FIVE: WHAT OBSTACLES MAY BLOCK YOU FROM KEEPING IT?

Keeping New Year's resolutions is notoriously more difficult than making them. The fifth card in this spread can help the querent keep his resolution by revealing potential problems for which he then may prepare himself. Yet to access this card's message we must see beyond the problems it indicates. We also must figure out how such problems may block the querent from keeping his resolution. For example, the reversed Two of Cups suggests a wide range of possible problems, but in Don Juan's reading, it was its indication of passion divorced from love and of illicit love affairs that seemed most likely to represent obstacles to his ability to develop a meaningful relationship.

Although revealing problems can help, it may not be enough though. If possible, we should try to find advice in card 5 for overcoming these obstacles, as was demonstrated in this section's reading. After all, every problem contains the seeds for its own solution if we dig deeply enough.

POSITION SIX: WHAT ARE THE PROBABLE RESULTS OF KEEPING THIS RESOLUTION?
The final card in this spread—the outcome card—brings the reading to a climax, and its interpretation depends on all that has gone before it. For example, in Don Juan's reading, the relevance of the innocent love implicit in the Six of Cups was explained in light of the King of Cups's message of emotional maturity. In addition, there was an explicit comparison between the Six of Cups and the obstacle card, the reversed Two of Cups, via the similarity of their imagery.

However, even when the other cards are not explicitly referenced in the explanation of card 6, their messages should be kept in mind as a foundation for understanding the probable outcome. Above all, though, card 1's suggested New Year's resolution should be related to the probable results indicated by card 6, for this outcome is the ultimate justification for the querent's resolution.

Other Notes About This Spread

Card 1 is the axis upon which a reading with this spread rotates. The other five cards expand upon its message, and their meanings depend upon it for their basis. However, there are other card relationships in this spread that can add texture and depth to our interpretation of this spread.

Cards 2 and 3 (hopes and fears) are often closely related. For example, we often fear the very things we hope for, and sometimes our hopes arise from a desire to overcome that which we fear. Thus, these two cards may be interpreted in light of each other. In Don Juan's reading, for example, they were compared explicitly in order to uncover the querent's primary concerns about making his resolution.

The final three cards are interrelated as well. The interpretation of the fourth card (reasons for the resolution) may benefit from a consideration of its relationship with cards 5 (obstacles) and 6 (results), and vice versa. To do so, we may explore questions such as,

How might the obstacles to keeping this resolution evolve out of the reasons for it? Does the probable outcome result from the reasons? Does it help explain the reasons?

Similarly, the obstacles and probable outcome may be explored more fully by comparing and contrasting the fifth and sixth cards. For example, does the probable outcome of card 6 indicate a solution to the obstacles of card 5? We also can think about what obstacles indicated by card 5 might block the anticipated results in card 6.

Finally, card 5 may be interpreted in light of cards 2 and 3. Obviously, the obstacles that the querent faces may arise from his fears, but ironically, they may have a basis in his hopes as well, especially if the benefits he desires contradict the probable results of making his resolution.

Alternative Spread

There is an expanded version of the New Year's Resolution spread that can yield an effective reading for a couple. It may be used on the couple's anniversary as well as at the beginning of the calendar year. This variation involves dealing two cards in each of the original spread's positions two through six. This results in an eleven-card spread, as indicated in Figure 24.

To use this spread, first deal one card to suggest a resolution for the couple, and ask both of them what resolution they see in this card.[25] They may decide to make one joint resolution, or one of them may find one resolution in this card while the other decides to use a variant of it.

For each of the remaining five positions from the original spread (hopes, fears, reasons, obstacles, and probable outcome), both parties should pull one card, which results in an "A" card for one person and a "B" card for the other. In addition to exploring the messages of their individual cards in these positions, it can be illuminating to compare and contrast each pair of A and B cards. Thus, for example, one person's hopes about the resolution can be examined relative to the other person's hopes about it.

One caveat about using this expanded New Year's Resolution spread, however, is to be sure to use it only when both members of the couple are present. Otherwise, it may be abused with the intent of violating the absent member's privacy.

---

25. It is desirable for both parties to be involved in the selection of this card. For example, one might shuffle the deck and the other might pick the card.

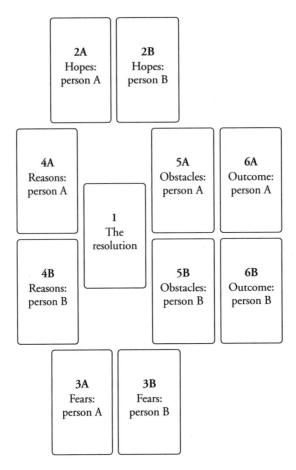

Figure 24. The Couple's Resolution spread.

THE PERSONAL
TRANSFORMATION SPREAD
A Six-Card Spread

I originally developed this spread to do readings in support of my fiction writing. More specifically, I wanted it to explore the lessons that a character needs to learn from a crisis or nexus point in his life. However, as I used this spread, I saw how well suited it is to the problems and dilemmas of real people too, which illustrates that fact that we can design a spread for one specific intention and then find that it also works well in other applications.

For this spread, I wanted several positions that would address the issue at hand from different points of view, so for inspiration, I considered the meanings of the basic types of Tarot cards: Aces, pips, court cards, and the major arcana.

The pip cards (cards 2 through 10 in the four suits) address the mundane events in our lives, so I wanted the first position to be about *what* is happening in the querent's life. The court cards usually concern people and personality traits, so I made the next position be about *who* the querent is. The Aces hold the purest essence of their suit, so each one can indicate the fundamental aspect of our lives that is associated with its suit. Because of that, I wanted there to be a position showing *where* the querent's problems or issues were having the greatest impact in his or her life. Finally, two important aspects of the major arcana cards are their spiritual lessons and the psychological archetypes they portray, so I created another position to ask *why* (on a psychospiritual level) the querent is experiencing this problem.[26] With all of this in mind, it seemed appropriate to separate the deck into these four kinds of cards in order to deal one from each type to its associated position. (The mechanics of this technique, which is uncommon but not unprecedented, will be described later.)

I also wanted to help the querent out of the dilemma, so I created two more positions, which should be selected from the entire deck. These positions deal with the querent's next step and its probable outcome.

The concepts outlined above led me to the spread used for this section's reading. They are, however, general and flexible enough that there are many other ways to use them in order to define spread positions. One such possibility is described under the heading of "Alternative Spreads" at the end of this section.

Considering the intention of its six positions, the Personal Transformation spread is equipped to help people face difficult situations. Thus, it can be used in readings when a querent has an "I just don't know what to do!" type of question and more than a quick fix is needed. In such situations, there often is a reason deeply rooted in the querent's psyche for his or her problems, as if the universe wants him or her to learn something from them. In support of this, the Personal Transformation spread examines the lesson that the querent needs to learn, because if the querent does not learn it, sooner or later he or she will be faced with it again (although it may be disguised as a new problem).

The Spread

Separate the deck into the following four stacks.

Type	Position
Pips (minor arcana cards 2–10)	Card 1
Court cards	Card 2
Major arcana cards	Card 3
Aces	Card 4

---

26. When I designed the layout for these cards, I switched the order of the Ace position and the major arcana position because it made more sense to examine the lesson to be learned before looking at what part of the querent's life that lesson was affecting most.

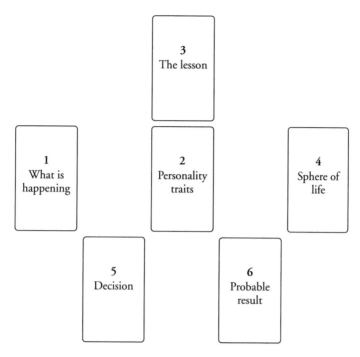

Figure 25. The Personal Transformation spread.

1. Shuffle each stack individually.

2. Deal the cards from the stacks as noted above into the positions indicated in Figure 25.

3. Shuffle all the remaining cards together again and deal cards 5 and 6.

Interpret these cards using the following positional definitions:

1. What do you need to understand about what is happening around you right now? (pip card)

2. What personality traits of yours are in need of reevaluation? (court card)

3. What is the lesson to be learned from your situation? (major arcana)

4. In what sphere of life is your lesson to be learned? (Ace)

5. What important decision will you need to make? (full deck)

6. What is the probable result of your decision? (full deck)

A KnightHawk Reading with the Personal Transformation Spread

Dear KnightHawk,

A certain business opportunity may be open to me, but I am wary of its moral implications. I have been told, however, that taking this course of action would be for the good of my people as well as being profitable for me, but I wonder about that. I am confused. What should I do?

Sincerely,
Judas Iscariot

*   *   *

Dear Judas,

Thank you for this opportunity to do a Tarot reading for you. It sounds like you have found yourself in an ethical dilemma, so I have dealt the following cards to see what insights the cards can give us about your situation and about where you may be going from here.

1. What do you need to understand about what is happening around you right now?
   Five of Swords reversed

2. Which of your personality traits are in need of reevaluation?
   Page of Wands reversed

3. What is the lesson to be learned from your situation?
   The Tower reversed

4. In what sphere of life is your lesson to be learned?
   Ace of Swords

5. What important decision will you need to make?
   The Hanged Man reversed

6. What is the probable result of your decision?
   Six of Swords

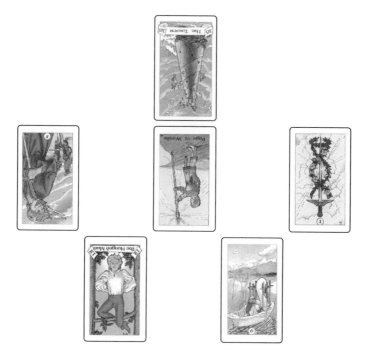

First of all, I am struck by the fact that among the minor arcana cards in this reading, there are no Cups or Pentacles cards, and three out of four of them are Swords cards. The general implication of this is that in your life right now, there is too little heart and grounding, and too much ego, conflict, and rationalization in your struggle for you to find your way.

Let us now turn to the individual cards here. The reversed Five of Swords holds rather dire implications regarding what is going on around you. It indicates that there are hidden motivations ranging from a conflict of opinions to malice, treachery, and intolerance. I also see that someone or some group is striving to assert its superiority, perhaps by trying to gain something from the misfortune of someone else. It is important, then, that as you consider your business opportunity, you try to achieve a clearer understanding of these covert motives, which may be based on deep-seated fears. You may be entering into a transaction wherein you seem to win, but ultimately you will lose much, for this seems to be a no-win situation that easily could lead to remorse and regret. This warning is emphasized by the fact that when reversed, the Five of Swords is more likely than usual to indicate that you erroneously are seeing someone else as being in the wrong, probably due to your ego trying to assert both itself and its position.

The Page of Wands can be about having a zealous nature, acting on impulse, and being driven by naïve ambition. However, since this card is reversed, it says that your zeal and ambition may be misguided. You may have had a flash of inspiration, but are acting on it without properly evaluating it or its consequences. Thus, this card urges you to see if you are being too rash, impetuous, or impatient in your consideration of this business opportunity. Finally, this card also may be a warning against being a messenger of bad news.

The lesson to be learned in this situation involves your ego and pride. The lesson of the Tower is humility, although the reversed aspect of this card implies that you may have a hard time seeing that or learning this lesson. More specifically, this card says that acting upon the dictates of your ego can easily betray you and guide you into a course of action that is erroneous or unjustified. Moreover, this business deal can have disastrous results that will be humbling, but eventually they may lead you to a new and more enlightened understanding of your situation or of your life in general.

The Ace of Swords says that the lesson of the Tower will affect your belief system and your plans and goals. Consequently, this card recommends a humble reexamination of your beliefs, which may then lead you to better reasoning and more clarity of thought in your business dealings.

The Hanged Man has been associated with traitors, and thus with betrayal, but it also can mean self-sacrifice or the sacrifice of material gain for spiritual awareness. Thus, this card implies that you face a decision between betraying someone (perhaps in order to make a profit) and sacrificing your own good for that of others or for a higher, more spiritual benefit. Being reversed, however, this card implies that you are leaning toward the more materialistic choice. Also, this card suggests that you think you are doing the right thing, but in viewing this situation from an orthodox point of view, you are not seeing some underlying truths about it. For example, as you focus on the material aspects of the issue at hand, you are missing the more important spiritual aspects. Therefore, this card urges you to look at your decision from a new point of view.

Another way of looking at the Hanged Man is to see it as a card of atonement. In that case, based on some of the messages of the previous cards (especially the warning of remorse and regret implicit in the reversed Five of Swords), I see the reversal of this card as meaning that this atonement will be delayed and difficult. Although this may take a while, or seemingly come too late, the Hanged Man does hold the promise of a spiritual turning point for you, especially if you eventually can surrender yourself to a higher power.

The probable outcome of the decision you face is depicted in the Six of Swords, whose interpretation is strongly affected by the card that precedes it, the reversed Hanged Man. This final card of your reading shows you in search of a new understanding, such as the altered point of view advised by the Hanged Man, as you try to leave behind troubled circumstances in search of peace. This quest for tranquility and deeper meaning in your life also may involve a spiritual passage for you. The general feeling of this card is one of serenity, which, although it is tinged with sorrow, suggests that you will at last incorporate the Hanged Man into your life.

In conclusion, the primary message that I get from this reading is its advice to slow down. Beware of rushing into this business venture, for there seem to be hidden, duplicitous motivations here. Try to uncover them so that you can act with wisdom and compassion, and avoid a possibly calamitous result. Also, reevaluate your own motives. Has your ego tainted them? Have the materialistic aspects of this venture blinded you to the more essential spiritual ones? But above all else, try to see this situation from a new perspective. If you do end up making a decision that has dire consequences, though, make amends and seek atonement in order that you may find peace.

Thank you for requesting this reading. I hope it helps you.

Best of luck,
KnightHawk

Comments on a Reading with the Personal Transformation Spread

The subject for this section's reading was suggested to me by Rachel Pollack, but I put off taking her suggestion for over a year because it posed quite a challenge. There is very little written about Judas in the Bible (the primary source of information about him), so I had to make a basic assumption in order to set the background for this reading. That assumption was that he was not entirely craven and that he did some soul-searching prior to executing his infamous betrayal. I based this interpretation of his character on his subsequent remorse, as noted in Matthew 27:3–5. Still, I approached this reading with a bit of trepidation, unsure if the paucity of information about this notorious figure might hamper my ability to interpret his reading within the context of his life and times.

As I dealt the cards, however, they all spoke clearly to me, and none more so than the Hanged Man. That card was amazingly appropriate on many levels: from Judas's traitorous betrayal to his need to find a new, more spiritual point of view; from him setting up Jesus to be the ultimate example of self-sacrifice to him becoming the Hanged Man in the literal sense. Some readings include a card that conveys an eerie literalism, but this one went a step beyond that. The Hanged Man was so obviously the perfect card turning up in exactly the right position that once I saw it, I no longer doubted the inspiration of Pollack's suggestion or the appropriateness of doing this reading.

Judas's name is equated with the terms *betrayal* and *traitor* to the extent that this one aspect of his life totally eclipses all others. Yet since I assumed that there was a spark of decency within him prior to his treachery, I also wondered if there was more to his ultimate fate than merely a cowardly escape via suicide. This reading ended up addressing that question in the outcome card (the Six of Swords) and, ironically, also in the first card in the spread (the reversed Five of Swords).

In *The Complete Book of Tarot Reversals*, Mary K. Greer makes the following comment about the reversed Five of Swords: "This is one of the few cards traditionally interpreted the same when reversed as when upright, with the added sense of *mourning after carnage or burials*." (Emphasis mine.) She then goes on to say, ". . . this card reflects the potential for spiritual growth after loss and sorrow."[27] When we additionally consider the potential for spiritual enlightenment in the Hanged Man, we can see in the somber—perhaps even sacred—passage depicted in the Six of Swords that maybe there was still an opportunity for atonement and redemption for Judas. Thus, this reading suggests that he was a tragic figure who played his villainous part in a divine drama, and in paying the ultimate price for it, he tried to atone for his actions.

Specific Notes About Individual Positions in the Spread

The first four positions in this spread focus on the archetypal questions of what, who, where, and why with the intention of helping the querent learn from his problems. The final two cards take him forward into the future and seek to help him make a decision and take action to resolve those problems.

---

27. Greer, *Complete Book of Tarot Reversals*, 146–47.

POSITION ONE: WHAT DO YOU NEED TO UNDERSTAND ABOUT WHAT IS HAPPENING AROUND YOU RIGHT NOW?

The first card in this spread, which is drawn from the pip cards in the minor arcana, concerns *what* is happening, thereby setting the scene in which the drama of the querent's life is being acted out. Generally, this card's message is directly applicable to the querent's concerns. Sometimes, however, it may discuss peripheral facets of his life, which, when taken in the context of the reading, may affect his stated problem.

POSITION TWO: WHICH OF YOUR PERSONALITY TRAITS ARE IN NEED OF REEVALUATION?

The card in this position is concerned with the querent's personality—that is, *who* he is. Although the definition of this position asks the querent to reevaluate the traits that it highlights, this does not necessarily mean that he must change them; merely that he should examine them closely. This process of self-examination will make him more aware of those characteristics and their consequences, but how he acts upon that expanded awareness is his choice. In fact, just being more aware of who he really is may be sufficient to improve how he handles the problems and choices he faces. Consequently, it is important that we avoid making value judgments as we examine the characteristics depicted in this second card.

POSITION THREE: WHAT IS THE LESSON TO BE LEARNED FROM YOUR SITUATION?

The third card, chosen from the major arcana, reveals *why*, on a spiritual or deeply psychological level, the querent has found himself mired in his problematic situation. The major arcana cards can be deep and complex, and encompass a wide range of meanings. However, their most pertinent aspects in this position are their depiction of archetypal energies deep within our psyches and important milestones along our soul's journey through life. Thus, what they usually reveal here are the psychospiritual lessons that are paramount in the querent's life at this time, and that is the aspect we should focus on when we interpret card 3.

POSITION FOUR: IN WHAT SPHERE OF LIFE IS YOUR LESSON TO BE LEARNED?

The fourth position asks *where* the lesson of the previous card is to be learned. This card is picked from the four Aces in the deck, which means that the lesson may be in the realm of the will or spirit (Wands), the emotions or relationships (Cups), beliefs or ideas (Swords), or the body or material resources (Pentacles). As a result, this card focuses the message of the third card via our interpretation of the suit of the Ace that is drawn. For example, in the reading for Judas, where the Tower indicated the lesson of humility, the Ace of Wands could have implied that he needed to make his will subservient to someone else's, the Ace of Cups might have said that his ego was blocking his ability to love, or the Ace of Pentacles may have meant that he had to learn to be less arrogant in his financial dealings. As it was, the Ace of Swords recommended that he make a humble reexamination of his beliefs.

POSITION FIVE: WHAT IMPORTANT DECISION WILL YOU NEED TO MAKE?

As noted at the beginning of this section, a primary intention of the Personal Transformation spread is to help the querent deal with the dilemmas and difficult situations he gets into and thereby transform himself and his life in the process. Since our actions are born of the choices we make, the fifth position in this spread addresses the querent's next big decision in order to help him act correctly as he moves forward with his life. Sometimes the card in this position comments on the alternatives that the querent faces, and sometimes it tries to help him choose between them. In either case, the decision is his, but at least this card's message will help him make a more informed choice.

POSITION SIX: WHAT IS THE PROBABLE RESULT OF YOUR DECISION?

The card in the last position discusses the possible consequences of the decision noted in card 5, so it should be interpreted in light of that card. Card 6 generally depicts the probable future based on the flow of events that currently carry the querent along the course of his life. However, if there is advice in the fifth card, this sixth one may show where the querent can go if he takes that advice and alters his life's trajectory. In the reading for Judas, the Hanged Man did give him some guidance, but being reversed, it suggested that he would resist taking that advice. As a result, I saw the Six of Swords as indicating where Judas was headed at the time of the reading instead of where he might have gone if he had heeded the Hanged Man's counsel and changed direction.

Other Notes About This Spread

In any Tarot reading, each card should be interpreted within the broad context of the entire reading. This includes everything from the querent's question to the tone and meaning of the other cards, especially adjacent ones. In the Personal Transformation spread, though, there are two pairs of cards that are particularly important to interpret together.

Cards 3 and 4 (what is to be learned and what area of your life is affected by the lesson) obviously influence each other. For example, important aspects of the Tower card, the third card in Judas's reading, include its discussion of hubris versus humility and its metaphorical depiction of the destruction of a rigid belief structure that can accompany a crisis. Consequently, in my interpretation of card 4 (the Ace of Swords), I focused on Judas's ambition, which is tied to ego issues, and his beliefs.

Cards 5 and 6 also should be interpreted together. In the reading for Judas, I saw a message about atonement in the Hanged Man due to the sense of a spiritual passage in the Six of Swords, and that interpretation of the Six of Swords was influenced by the spiritual tone of the Hanged Man. So, which came first: my interpretation of the Hanged Man or my understanding of the Six of Swords? Neither. I got a sense of the messages of both cards as I viewed the two of them together.

Alternative Spreads

As noted at the beginning of this section, the concepts behind the six positions in this spread lend themselves to many possible positional definitions. An example of this is the following alternate definition for the Personal Transformation spread.

1. What do you need to do at this time in your life? (pip card)

2. Whose actions are primarily affecting you? (court card)

3. What important milestone are you dealing with at this time in your life? (major arcana)

4. In what sphere of life do you face your greatest challenge? (Ace)

5. What action will you need to take in order to resolve your problem? (full deck)

6. Where might this action lead you? (full deck)

You may choose to use this one instead of the one used in this section's reading, or you may create your own alternative spread that restates the following generic questions for these six positions:

1. What?

2. Who?

3. Why?

4. Where?

5. How?

6. Probable outcome?

Another alternative, albeit a minor one, involves the selection of the cards for the Personal Transformation spread. Considering the specific intent of the first four positions, I decided to sort the deck into types of cards prior to dealing them. However, some people prefer to use the entire deck for each position, and this provides a slight variation to the use of this spread.

If a quicker reading is required, we may want to use an abbreviated version of the Personal Transformation spread consisting of cards 1 through 4. On the other hand, if a longer reading is possible or if more depth seems needed, a nine-card Expanded Personal Transformation spread may be used. This expansion, which is described below, incorporates some of the alternative positional definitions noted above.

Again, the first step in using the Expanded Personal Transformation spread is to separate the deck into four stacks. The following table defines which cards should come from which stacks. (Note that the cards dealt from each stack differ slightly from the assignments defined for the Personal Transformation spread.)

Type	*Position*
Pips (minor arcana cards 2–10)	Card 1
Court cards	Card 3
Major arcana cards	Cards 2 and 4
Aces	Card 5

1. Shuffle each stack individually.

2. Deal the cards from the stacks as noted above into the positions indicated in Figure 26.

3. Shuffle all the remaining cards back together and deal cards 6 through 9.

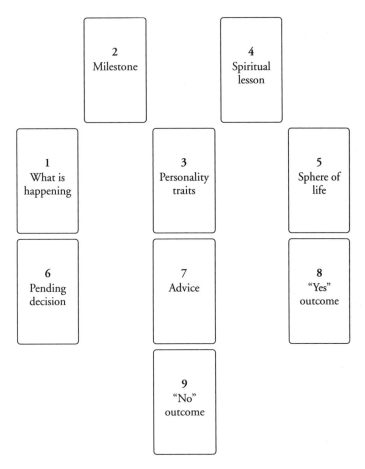

Figure 26. The Expanded Personal Transformation spread.

Interpret these cards using the following positional definitions:

1. What do you need to understand about what is going on in your life at this time? (pip card)

2. What important milestone are you dealing with right now? (major arcana)

3. What kind of person do you need to be to cope effectively with what is happening in your life? (court card)

4. What is the spiritual lesson in your current situation? (major arcana)

5. In what area of your life is there the greatest need or potential for growth at this time? (Ace)

6. What important decision are you facing now? (full deck)

7. How might you act upon this decision to create the greatest good in your life? (full deck)

8. What is the probable outcome if you follow the advice of card 7? (full deck)

9. What is the probable outcome if you ignore the advice of card 7? (full deck)

THE EXPANDED CHOICE SPREAD
An Eight-Card Spread

When asked to do a reading for a choice question (i.e., a question like, "Should I do this or should I do that?"), I often use a three-card choice spread. In such spreads, positions one and three may be defined as considerations about the two options that the querent faces, advantages or disadvantages of those options, or their probable outcomes. The middle position may be defined as a compromise or new alternative, or it may indicate some sort of advice or deciding factor that could help the querent decide between these two choices. Obviously, then, there are many different three-card spreads that we can devise based on this description. For example, we can define a three-card choice spread as:

1. Advantages of choice A

2. A compromise alternative

3. Advantages of choice B

Or we can define it as:

1. Probable outcome of choice A

2. A deciding factor

3. Probable outcome of choice B

Obviously there are many other possibilities as well. See the "Alternative Spreads" section of "The Decision Spread: A Three-Card Spread" for an extended discussion about three-card spreads.

This sort of spread works well for relatively quick readings, but sometimes we want to do a reading for a choice question that is longer and more involved, especially if it seems appropriate to explore in greater depth several of the options afforded by this type of spread. For such purposes, I have created a larger spread based on this type of three-card spread. It incorporates both "Considerations about . . ." and "Probable outcome of . . ." positions for the querent's two options, and for an alternative choice as well. I lay out the cards for these three options so that they radiate out in three directions from a focal card called "The background of your situation," which sets the stage for the whole reading. The result is the eight-card spread illustrated in Figure 27.

The Spread

Begin by dealing eight cards as indicated in Figure 27.

Interpret these cards using the following positional definitions:

1. The background of your situation

2. Considerations about option A

3. Considerations about option B

4. A new alternative (called option C), which may be a compromise between options A and B.

5. Considerations about option C

6. Probable outcome of option A

7. Probable outcome of option B

8. Probable outcome of option C

A KnightHawk Reading with the Expanded Choice Spread

Dear KnightHawk,

I am torn between two men. Edgar Linton has proposed to me, and I am inclined to accept his proposal, for the civility and luxury of his estate, Thrushcross Grange, is quite

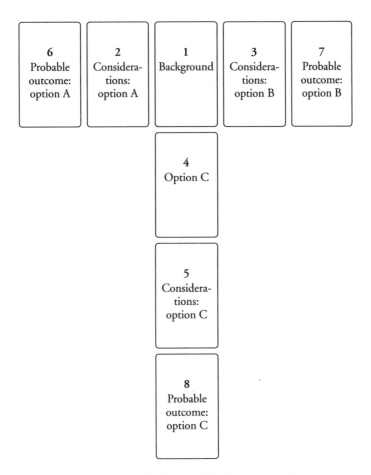

Figure 27. The Expanded Choice spread.

appealing. But it is Heathcliff I truly love. However, since my brother has made Heathcliff his servant here at Wuthering Heights, it would degrade me to marry him, wouldn't it?
    Which man shall I choose: Edgar Linton or Heathcliff? Please help me decide.

Affectionately,
Catherine Earnshaw

*   *   *

Dear Miss Earnshaw,

    Thank you for requesting my help in making this difficult decision. I have asked the cards to explain and clarify the options you face and to present and explore a

new alternative for you as well. This will help you make a decision that should serve you well. In pursuit of this enlightenment, the cards I dealt are these:

1. The background of your situation:
   King of Swords

2. Considerations about marrying Edgar Linton:
   Temperance

3. Considerations about marrying Heathcliff:
   Two of Swords reversed

4. A third option:
   Four of Pentacles

5. Considerations about that third option:
   Queen of Wands

6. Probable outcome of marrying Edgar Linton:
   Six of Wands

7. Probable outcome of marrying Heathcliff:
   Ace of Wands reversed

8. Probable outcome of the third option:
   Ace of Pentacles

The first card in this spread, the King of Swords, may indicate someone affecting your life, or it may be an aspect of your own personality. As someone in your life, it depicts a person in a position of authority who you feel is blocking your path. This is probably your brother, but I do not think he means you harm. Instead, I think he is exercising his power in an attempt to protect you and to keep you from making a mistake, even though he may be acting in a severe and autocratic manner. If, on the other hand, we consider this card to be commenting on you, it says that you are inclined to make the decision that you face based on a rational assessment that ignores the dictates of your heart. It is up to you, of course, to decide whether or not this is a wise course, but perhaps the other cards in this spread will help you make this decision.

Now let us examine the two choices for which you have requested this reading. First, the Temperance card says that the primary consideration about a relationship with Edgar Linton is that life with him would be balanced and moderate. Typically this man is temperate in his demeanor and in his desires, and so your marriage would be calm and staid. If this is what you want, he may suit you well.

The reversed Two of Swords, however, says that choosing Heathcliff will result in a stormy, tempestuous relationship. For one thing, it probably would lead to discord with your brother, but more than that, whatever harmony you may hope to find with Heathcliff may be illusory or troubled. Thus, the advice of this card is that you will need to cultivate your own sense of internal peace in order to cope with this relationship. Also, to establish a truce within the conflicts that are potential in this relationship, you sometimes may need to turn a blind eye to Heathcliff's shortcomings, which probably will be hard for you to do.

Besides these two options, however, there is a third alternative that perhaps you have not considered. The Four of Pentacles suggests that you do not have to pick either of these suitors. You may choose no one, deciding instead to live on your own, thereby finding or establishing your own security and stability. You might think this option offers only loneliness, which you may find unattractive, but let us look at other considerations about it as we turn to the next card.

The Queen of Wands is a cheerful and radiant card, and it suggests that this third option could help you discover who you really are and find the joy within you. It acknowledges your passion for life and your strength of character, as well as your wild, impetuous nature. It says that if you decide to find your own way in life, you will be able to develop, refine, and manifest those bright characteristics. This card also suggests that this option will allow you more control over your life, or it may even give you control over Wuthering Heights. It sees you developing courage and optimism, but it warns against allowing yourself to become domineering or overbearing as well.

Let us turn now to the probable outcome for each of these three choices. First, the Six of Wands tells us that marriage to Edgar Linton may seem to be a victory for you, bringing you the things you want and the life you desire, but along the way, it also may require you to bridle your passions. In addition, this card warns against becoming prideful of all that you may gain through this marriage. Remember and appreciate the people who have cared about you and supported you along the way, including both your brother and Heathcliff.

Next, the Ace of Wands is a card of great power and vitality, but its message is made ominous by its reversed aspect here. It says that Heathcliff's desire and ardor could become destructive as it is consumed by the shadowy aspects of his obsessions. Thus, a relationship with him probably would be dominated by self-centered passions, including intense jealousy, and you may find yourself overpowered by his indomitable will. In that case, the advice of this card is that you would need to develop your inner strength and the power of your own self-esteem.

Finally, the Ace of Pentacles is a card of great fortune, perhaps indicating an inheritance (of Wuthering Heights, maybe?) that brings wealth and abundance. It depicts a future for you in which you are able to find a peaceful prosperity within the security of a comfortable home. In fact, the probable outcome of not marrying at all may be that you would be happy staying at Wuthering Heights, alone but fulfilled and satisfied with the simple beauty of your home and of the land on which you live.

Now that we have examined what each of these cards has to tell us individually, let us look at a few combinations of them. First, let's see what we can read here about the three options examined in this reading.

With regards to choosing Edgar Linton, consider cards 1, 2, and 6. These three cards tell a story wherein you rationally and dispassionately choose Edgar, and then find yourself in a relatively calm, peaceful marriage that brings you the success you seem to want, although you must reign in your passions to keep it.

Looking at cards 1, 3, and 7, we see that to choose Heathcliff, you must defy your brother's authority, but that choice will plunge you blindly into an unexpectedly conflicted relationship that easily may end up consuming itself in dysfunctional passions.

In cards 1, 4, 5, and 8, we read a tale in which choosing neither man will require you to remain with your stern brother—a safe but seemingly lonely option. This choice, however, eventually can transform you into a bright, optimistic, and independent woman and then lead you to the quiet joy of a comfortable and secure life.

Now let us compare the considerations about each option and the probable outcomes for them. Turning first to cards 2, 3, and 5, it seems that the difference between Edgar Linton and Heathcliff is one of stability. Marriage to Edgar would be rather staid, whereas with Heathcliff your life would be tumultuous, constantly requiring you to struggle to find and maintain your equilibrium. The third option, on the other hand, is all about you. Its promise is for you to actualize your highest and brightest potential.

Moving on to cards 6, 7, and 8, it is in the level of passion in these relationships that we see a contrast between the probable outcome of marrying Edgar Linton versus that of marrying Heathcliff. With Edgar, the passion of your marriage would be bridled, whereas with Heathcliff, it would be hard to manage, or it even may go awry. If you choose to marry no one, the probable outcome would be prosperous, serene, and secure.

Thank you for requesting this reading, Miss Earnshaw. I hope that these insights into the choices you face will help you make the best decision possible.

Best of luck to you,
KnightHawk

Comments on a Reading with the Expanded Choice Spread

For the sake of those who are not familiar with *Wuthering Heights,* the following is a brief overview of the story.

This tale begins when Catherine Earnshaw is a young girl and her father brings Heathcliff, an orphaned boy, into their home and raises him as one of his children. Mr. Earnshaw even comes to prefer this boy over his own son, Hindley, who consequently resents Heathcliff. Catherine and Heathcliff, however, are kindred souls and love being together.

After Mr. Earnshaw's death, Hindley sets out to degrade Heathcliff and to crush his spirit, but Catherine remains loyal to him—that is, until she meets the wealthy Linton family, whose civility and luxury seduce her. So when Edgar Linton proposes to her, she accepts.

Although Heathcliff's material fortunes subsequently rise, his soul languishes as he becomes obsessed with seeking revenge for the loss of the woman he loves. As he vies for Catherine's affections, she becomes torn between two worlds and suffers as a consequence. She dies young, immediately after bearing a daughter, but Heathcliff lives on miserably until at last he is able to rejoin her in death.

I had always assumed that Heathcliff's unhappiness was caused by his loss of Catherine Earnshaw, but this reading indicated that the fundamental cause of his doom was his obsession with her. The reversed Ace of Wands indicated that his love and passion for her was selfish and self-centered, which was reflected in the book when he refused to forgive her at the end of her life. Subsequently, his obsession with Catherine fueled his insatiable lust for revenge, and now I see that even if he had not lost her, that same obsession easily could have blinded him with jealousy, and their relationship would have been consumed in the flames of their passion. Although Catherine's choice of Edgar Linton proved to be an unhappy one, this reading implied that choosing Heathcliff could have been disastrous for her.[28]

---

28. It is important to remember that this reading was for Catherine, not Heathcliff. He probably would have preferred a tumultuous, even abusive, marriage to her instead of the wretched life he lived without her.

Specific Notes About Individual Positions in the Spread

POSITION ONE: THE BACKGROUND OF YOUR SITUATION

The first card in this spread can provide background information regarding the choices the querent faces, or it can comment on her general attitude and mindset in her approach to this decision. In the reading for Catherine Earnshaw, the card in this position was a court card, which was able to do both since it could be seen as either someone influencing her life or an aspect of her personality.

POSITIONS TWO, THREE, AND FIVE: CONSIDERATIONS . . .

The considerations that these three cards point out should be viewed as the primary considerations that the querent should keep in mind as she seeks to make her decision. For example, the fact that marriage to Edgar Linton could turn out to be "balanced and moderate . . . calm and staid" should have been a major concern for Catherine Earnshaw since she was so vibrant, impulsive, and willful. Instead, she made her choice based on her desire for wealth and social standing, factors that do not play a part in card 2, the Temperance card. Of course, the shortcomings of a relationship with Heathcliff that this reading revealed might have made marriage to him seem to be an even less viable alternative.

POSITION FOUR: A THIRD OPTION

The new option presented by card 4 may be a compromise between the other two choices, or it may be a completely new alternative. It can be unexpected or surprising, or it can be an option the querent was aware of but had not taken seriously before.

The Four of Pentacles in this section's reading suggested an alternative (the voluntary renunciation of marriage) that Catherine probably had not considered, and that she may have found unthinkable due to the culture in which she had been raised. Nevertheless, other cards in this reading imply that ultimately she may have found it to be the most preferable option.

POSITIONS SIX, SEVEN, AND EIGHT: PROBABLE OUTCOME . . .

As always, an outcome indicated in a Tarot reading should be considered probable, not definite. After all, even if the prediction is dire, forewarned is forearmed. On the other hand, when the querent is shown an outcome that appears rosy, there is a danger that she may become complacent, thereby allowing a potentially bright future to slip through her fingers. In either case, with knowledge of three alternative possible futures, the querent will be in a better position to see which direction to take and to prepare herself for what lies ahead on whichever path she chooses. Remember, however, that ultimately we can only illuminate the path ahead; it is up to the querent herself to pick which direction to take in order to make her own future.

Other Notes About This Spread

As noted in "The Lovers Card Spread: A Nine-Card Spread," most spreads having more than a few cards contain several subspreads. These clusters of cards can be viewed as a small spread (generally of about three or four cards) that is easier to work with than the complete spread, while still providing a context within which the cards can speak and interact with each other. They also provide an intermediate layer of meaning that serves as a bridge between individual card interpretations and the overall message for the reading.

To find subspreads, it is useful to look for cards that are related in such a way that they make up a logical sequence, imply a familiar spread (such as the Past, Present, Future spread, for example), or share a common theme. The subspreads used in the reading for Catherine Earnshaw were of two types: cards that form a logical sequence applicable to one of her options, and cards that share a common theme (considerations or probable outcome) regarding each of her options.

Exploration of the sequence subspreads (cards 1, 2, and 6; cards 1, 3, and 7; and cards 1, 4, 5, and 8) can provide a review and summarization of each of the querent's options, and also yield additional insights into them. When looked at as a series of illustrations for a story, the cards within these sequences often fall into place like pieces of a puzzle, and their meanings are clarified as a result.

In this section's reading, a comparison of these three clusters helped me see that choosing Heathcliff seemed to be the most ominous of Catherine's options. The fact that the only reversed cards in this reading occurred within the sequence relevant to that choice, and that the preponderance of the cards in the Heathcliff sequence were in that problematic aspect, helped me arrive at that conclusion.

The first comparison subspread (cards 2, 3, and 5) focuses attention on considerations about the querent's various options, while the second one (cards 6, 7, and 8) focuses on their probable outcomes. In making these comparisons, we can find new insights about each card by contrasting it with the other cards in its subspread. For example, the Two of Swords can be about decisions and compromise, but it also talks about balance. Comparing this card with the Temperance card, which has a strong aspect of balance as well, showed me that balance was a key factor in choosing between these two men. This led me to say that the reversed Two of Swords implied that marriage to Heathcliff would require her "to struggle to find and maintain [her] equilibrium."

Alternative Spreads

When I created the Expanded Choice spread, I used "Considerations about . . ." in positions two, three, and five instead of "Advantages of . . ." (or "Disadvantages of . . .") because I thought "Considerations about . . ." was more flexible. Alternatively, we might prefer to use "Advantages of . . ." in those three positions, but actually, we do not have to make that choice. We can use both "Considerations" and "Advantages" if we add three more positions to the spread in order to cover the advantages of each option. In addition, we can add a position to comment specifically on a deciding factor to help the querent make her decision. With those changes made, the Expanded Choice spread would become a twelve-card spread, as illustrated in Figure 28. Its cards may be interpreted using the following positional definitions:

1. Background of your situation

2. Considerations about option A

3. Advantages of option A

4. Considerations about option B

5. Advantages of option B

6. A new alternative (called option C), which may be a compromise between options A and B

7. Considerations about option C

8. Advantages of option C

9. Probable outcome of option A

10. Probable outcome of option B

11. Probable outcome of option C

12. A deciding factor to help make this decision

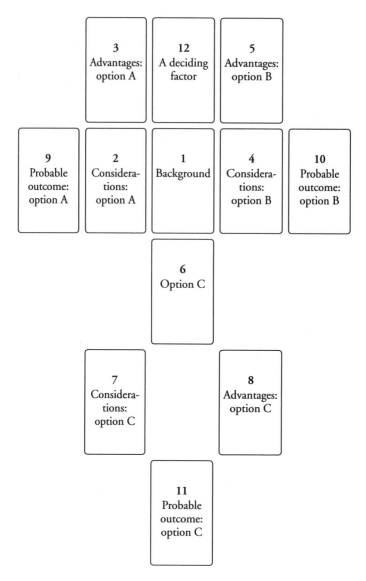

Figure 28. The Fully Expanded Choice spread.

THE FAILURE'S ALCHEMY SPREAD
A Nine-Card Spread

As noted in "The Sorrow's Alchemy Spread: A Four-Card Spread," the idea for a Tarot spread can come from anywhere. For example, the inspiration for this section's spread came from an article in the *Los Angeles Times Magazine* about people who found success after they had suffered defeat.[29] That article noted that while some people and some organizations are devastated and defeated by failure, others are able to learn from their mistakes, recover quickly, and go on to achieve success. It is how they respond to failure and how they deal with it that determines their ability to succeed in the future.

As I read this article, it struck me that many of the ideas presented in it could help my Tarot clients. Typically, people come for a reading when they are at a low point in their lives, and often they got there because of a recent failure—usually in their career or in a relationship. They typically ask for a reading to see if they will ever find success, but I prefer to use the Tarot to help people *create* a better future rather than to see if their probable future looks bright or bleak. Generally, people are pleasantly surprised to hear that a Tarot reading can do that, and they agree to let me focus the reading on advice and assistance. The Failure's Alchemy spread was designed to do just that.

As a first step in creating this spread, I reread the article mentioned above and took notes about some of the effective ways in which people can respond to failure in order to lay the groundwork for future success. From this, I created a list of concepts that could

---

29. Michael D'Antonio, "The Advantage of Falling Short," *L.A. Times Magazine,* July 14, 2002, 12.

define valuable positions in a spread, keeping in mind how each item might lend itself to a Tarot reading. After a bit of weeding and tweaking, I made a first pass at a list of positional meanings.

The next step was to put these items into some sort of meaningful order. First I tried to sort them by levels of being (such as mental, emotional, and physical), but that did not seem to work well. Then I put them into a somewhat chronological order, which suited the spread better. Although there was not an exact chronological sequence to the list, the items were basically sorted into three groupings: past, present, future. The resulting list is as follows:

1. What should you accept responsibility for?

2. What mistakes should you forgive yourself for?

3. What can you learn from this experience?

4. Where can you find help?

5. Where else in your life can you find fulfillment at this time?

6. What can you hope to salvage from this failure?

7. What can you do to set yourself on the road to recovery?

8. What can you do differently next time?

9. Where can you go from here? What new venture can you look forward to?

Finally, I considered what shape to use for this layout. My first idea was to use a geometric design. A nine-sided figure was too awkward, but what about an octagon with one card in the center? That looked better, but it did not seem to reflect the theme of the spread very well. So I tried to think of an image whose meaning would work well with the basic concept of this spread. I settled on a rainbow, since it captures the idea of finding something wonderful after experiencing difficulty—that is, the peace after a storm. Thus, I arranged the cards in an arch in order to represent a rainbow.

I modified the order of the positions and the shape of the spread a bit, however, because I intuited that two of the positions needed to be in a special place of their own. The ninth card especially begged to be placed "over the rainbow." In addition, separating out those two cards left seven cards for the arch of the rainbow, which felt right since rainbows traditionally are depicted having seven colors. This process led to the spread depicted in Figure 29.

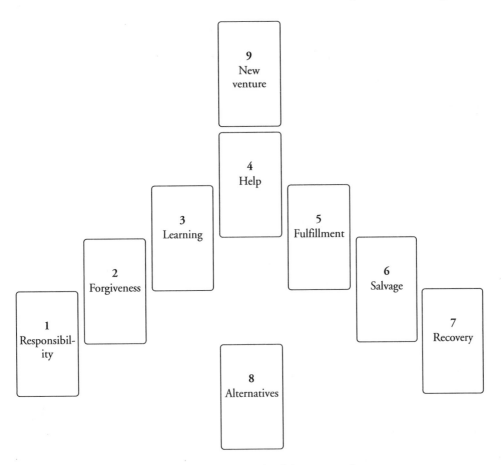

Figure 29. The Failure's Alchemy spread.

The Spread

Begin by dealing nine cards as indicated in Figure 29.

Interpret these cards using the following positional meanings:

1. What must you accept responsibility for?

2. What should you forgive yourself for?

3. What can you learn from this experience?

4. Where can you find help?

5. What can you hope to salvage from this failure?

6. What can you do to set yourself on the road to recovery?

7. What can you do differently next time?

8. Where else in your life can you find fulfillment at this time?

9. Where can you go from here, or what new venture can you look forward to?

A KnightHawk Reading with the Failure's Alchemy Spread

Dear Sir,

Events of the past few years regarding the issue of slavery have impelled me to return to politics, and this year, to seek election to the Senate in opposition to Senator Stephen A. Douglas. I thought I had a good chance of winning this election, but I lost. This race did allow me to speak out forcefully on the great and durable question of the age—slavery—but as a result of my defeat, I feel that I shall sink out of view and be forgotten. Is this the case? Will I yet find success in my political ambitions?

Sincerely,
Abraham Lincoln

*   *   *

Dear Mr. Lincoln,

Recovery from defeat is always a difficult process, but we all can learn from our failures and come back to achieve success. I have done the following Tarot reading to show you how you might do this and where you might look for achievement and victory in the future.

The cards I dealt for you are the following:

1. What must you accept responsibility for?
   Three of Swords

2. What should you forgive yourself for?
   Knight of Cups reversed

3. What can you learn from this experience?
   Page of Wands reversed

4. Where can you find help?
   The Tower

5. What can you hope to salvage from this failure?
   Seven of Wands

6. What can you do to set yourself on the road to recovery?
   Eight of Pentacles reversed

7. What can you do differently next time?
   Two of Cups

8. Where else in your life can you find fulfillment at this time?
   Queen of Swords

9. Where can you go from here, or what new venture can you look forward to? Three of Wands reversed

This reading begins with a somewhat troubling card: the Three of Swords. This card can indicate painful truths, words that hurt or that are divisive, and insights that cut to the heart of the matter. This implies that you must accept that your defeat may have been due to exhibiting an uncompromising attitude or to taking a position that presented painful truths that most people did not want to face. You may have cut to the heart of the matter, but with such an emotional issue as slavery, this can cause resentment in many. Note, however, that this card is concerned with responsibility, not blame. The opinions and observations you have expressed may have been too painful for some people to accept, but it is up to you to evaluate their correctness and whether or not it was right or appropriate to express them.

The next card, the reversed Knight of Cups, urges you to forgive yourself for allowing your emotions too much control over your actions. Maybe you succumbed to depression now and then, or perhaps you feel that you followed your heart too much and thus got lost in an emotionally charged cause. Although this card may recommend that you be more practical and follow your reason more in the future, it certainly does not mean that it is wrong to listen to your emotions or intuition sometimes too. So try to let go of blaming yourself for acting upon your intuition or the dictates of your heart, for eventually there may be a need for you to be something of a visionary.

Now let us see what you can learn from this experience. The Page of Wands is often about youthful energy, enthusiasm, and exuberance, but its reversal here moderates these interpretations. This seems to be another caution to be more grounded and practical in your future efforts, relying less on enthusiasm and more on realism. This card also urges you to temper your ambition for now with patience and caution. On the other hand, it does acknowledge the value of your enthusiasm. I see that it encourages you to realize and remember the importance of that characteristic in the face of adversity that may yet come your way, just be sure to moderate it with pragmatism.

The Tower is a very powerful and influential card, especially in this particular reading since it is the only major arcana card in the spread. This card deals with what can help you, and on a personal level, it says that your humility will help you in your future political pursuits. More importantly, however, this card has a more universal message. It reflects upon the precarious condition of the country at this time, saying that a national crisis is at hand. More than anything else, it is this crisis that will help bring you future success. This card also presages a sudden and drastic change that you can take advantage of by being flexible and adaptable. Maybe, then, it foretells the breakdown or sundering of a formidable organization that opposes you.

The next card, the Seven of Wands, shows us what you can salvage from your defeat. It says that you held your ground well in the 1858 Senatorial campaign. Your resolve was tested, as was your ability to hold your own in serious debate, so you proved your mettle. Thus, although you lost this election, you have established your reputation as a strong and worthy campaigner and politician, which will go a long way toward supporting your future success. Also, the Seven of Wands says that although you may have lost the election, this campaign has renewed and confirmed your inner convictions, so hold on to them.

While the Eight of Pentacles can indicate diligence, hard work, and keeping your nose to the grindstone, in this reading it is reversed. The most obvious interpretation of this reversal is that to set yourself on the road to recovery, you should relax, take a break, and get away from politics and work in general. A deeper message, however, may be that not being in public office now may be a blessing in disguise. For example, this might allow you to focus your attention on the steps required to move forward with your political career.

Next, the Two of Cups provides some advice for your future political efforts. First, it suggests taking a more conciliatory tone. Emphasize compromise and cooperation, either within your own party or with your opponents. It also stresses the importance of supportive relationships, urging you to expand your professional relationships or to strengthen existing ones. In addition, you may want to try to rely more on the cooperative support of others next time.

Before moving on to the final two cards in this spread, let me summarize the message of the first seven. These cards say that in your future efforts you should be firm and assertive, but also conciliatory and open to cooperation. In addition, have a clear vision of what you want, but that vision should be tempered with patience and practicality. The most important of these seven cards, however, is the Tower, which warns of an impending crisis. This emergency will have a strong determining influence on your fate, as it can benefit your aspirations, especially if you can meet it with resolution, diligence, flexibility, and a spirit of cooperation and reconciliation.

Let us now turn to the last two cards of this spread. In a Tarot reading, the court cards may indicate your personality traits, or they can depict someone else in your life. In the case of the Queen of Swords, I see your wife being indicated, which means that it is in your marriage that you can seek fulfillment at this time. This, of course, reinforces the message of the Eight of Pentacles, which said that you could use a break from your work. In addition, this card says that your wife's frank insights may be a valuable source of support at this time.

Finally, we come to the last card, the reversed Three of Wands. This card indicates that forces have been set in motion to carry you toward your destiny, but it will take time and perseverance before it comes to pass. So again, patience is advised. As to the nature of the venture toward which you can set your sights, it will be one of authority, leadership, and command. However, due to the reversed aspect of this card, it also seems that this enterprise may entail a great deal of risk and be both difficult and precarious. It will require foresight, which will be made harder by the fact that the future may appear uncertain and obscure at times, and it will entail the command of forces that sometimes seem beyond your control. Yet although there will be great risk, the rewards may be equally substantial.

In conclusion, I see that the path you face may be difficult, but the challenges ahead are ones that you will be able to master. Your past defeat should not impede your future success if you are prepared to weather the storms ahead, choosing your position carefully, standing your ground, and acting with compassion as well as vision. In the short term, however, a bit of rest is in order. Spend some time at home with your family, and then, when ready, you will be set to move ahead with your life and with your career.

Thank you for requesting this reading, Mr. Lincoln. I hope it helps you.

Best of luck to you,
KnightHawk

Comments on a Reading with the *Failure's Alchemy Spread*

If there was ever a shining example of personal victory rising from the ashes of defeat, it was the career of Abraham Lincoln. Lincoln served a single term as a congressman from Illinois (1847–1849), but he was not reelected. He then returned to his law practice until the increasingly heated and contentious debate over the issue of slavery rekindled his interest in politics. In 1856 he was considered for the vice presidential slot on the Republican ticket, but was not nominated. In 1858 he ran for the Senate against the incumbent, Stephen A. Douglas, but lost that election. Despite these defeats, he rose from being a dark horse candidate at the 1860 Republican national convention to be nominated as their presidential candidate and then to be elected president of the United States.

In the reading for Abraham Lincoln, the Tower card looms large as the central card in the spread and as the only major arcana card, which made it the lynchpin of the reading. Its message, however, was baffling at first until I realized that its most important message was not what it indicated about Lincoln personally, but what it said about the world in which he lived and the backdrop against which his future efforts would be played out. There is hardly a better card than the Tower to represent America in 1858: a house divided that was ripe for a disastrous crisis.

Although Lincoln's position on the abolition of slavery was moderate compared to that of many of his abolitionist contemporaries, Southern states, fearing he would free their slaves, began to secede from the Union almost immediately upon his election, even before he took office. However, the message of the Tower card is that a crisis was imminent no matter who had won the 1860 election. It was just the nature and timing of that crisis, along with its ultimate outcome, that hung in the balance. What this card reveals is that it was this inevitable crisis, which was already brewing in 1858, that created the remarkable Lincoln presidency. Had it not existed, it is likely that he would never have become president and would have faded into historical obscurity.

Specific Notes About Individual Positions in the Spread

Position One: What Must You Accept Responsibility For?

As noted in this section's reading, the card in position one is about responsibility, not about blame. This is an important distinction to make, since blame is neither productive nor creative. It mires us in past mistakes, whereas responsibility allows us to correct our mistakes, atone for them, and progress beyond them.

Also, what the querent should take responsibility for may or may not have been a mistake, although such an evaluation is for him to make. For example, the Lincoln-Douglas debates won national recognition for Lincoln, but they also labeled him as an abolitionist, which alienated him from much of his constituency in 1858. He had to assume responsibility for the effects of taking this position, but was it a mistake? Could he have, in good conscience, taken a less controversial position? Even then, would a more moderate position have helped him win the 1858 senatorial election? Consider also that although he lost that election, those debates probably help set the stage for his victory in the 1860 presidential election.

So, the meaning of this first position is subtler than it seems at first glance. It is not about blame, and in fact, it may not even be about a need to change something. The card in this position just points out that the querent should be conscious of what he has done and take responsibility for his actions so that he can reasonably evaluate them and decide how he may or may not want to modify them in the future. Also, if he can say, "Yes, I failed and it was because of this action I took. But I stand by it anyway, for it was the right thing to do," then perhaps he can at least feel better about himself and not let his defeat get him down.

POSITION TWO: WHAT SHOULD YOU FORGIVE YOURSELF FOR?
One of the worst things about experiencing defeat is our tendency to beat ourselves up about it afterward. We are all human, and we all make mistakes now and then, but it is hard to find healing and to move on with our lives unless we can forgive ourselves first. Also, we always have the potential to learn at least as much from failure as from success, but we cannot discover what value there may be in our setbacks while we are preoccupied with self-incrimination. So the card in this position focuses attention more on self-forgiveness than on the correction of mistakes.

POSITION THREE: WHAT CAN YOU LEARN FROM THIS EXPERIENCE?
After assuming responsibility and finding self-forgiveness, we are ready to learn from a difficult experience. Of course, there usually is much to learn from any failure, but the focus of the third position in this spread is on the more crucial or immediate lessons. In Lincoln's case, his defeat could have dampened his resolve and determination, so the reversed Page of Wands assured him that although he had to learn to "temper [his] ambition . . . with patience and caution," he also needed to hold on to his enthusiasm despite this discouraging setback.

POSITION FOUR: WHERE CAN YOU FIND HELP?
Typically, the help indicated by the card in the fourth position refers to a resource (either internal or external) that the querent can access, a favorable circumstance he can take advantage of, or someone who can assist, support, or guide him—or some combination of these three. In Lincoln's case, it depicted his humility (an internal resource), but more importantly, it pointed toward an impending national crisis (an external circumstance).

It is rare that so fateful a message will show up in a Tarot reading for an individual, but circumstances such as those behind the reading for Abraham Lincoln are rare as well.

An interesting side note about the Tower card being in this position concerns the literalisms that we can see in it. In accepting the Republican senatorial nomination in 1858, Lincoln delivered his famous speech in which he said that the conflict over the slavery issue "will not cease until a crisis shall have been reached and passed. A house divided against itself cannot stand." Surely, then, the image on the Tower card, which depicts a sundered house, would have reminded Lincoln of his warning. Also, as an initial manifestation of Lincoln's prediction, the Democratic party suffered a schism at their 1860 national convention, resulting in two Democrats running for president: a northerner, Stephen A. Douglas, and a southerner, John C. Breckinridge. Thus divided, the Democratic Party fell in the 1860 election like the lightning-struck Tower, and virtually handed Lincoln the presidency.

POSITION FIVE: WHAT CAN YOU HOPE TO SALVAGE FROM THIS FAILURE?
Few, if any, failures are total disasters, and there is almost always something that can be salvaged from one. At the very least, lessons can be learned from a defeat, but in addition, something of value often comes out of it as well. For example, in Lincoln's reading, the Seven of Wands said that what he could salvage from his 1858 senatorial defeat was his proven resolve, his good reputation as a campaigner and politician, even under daunting circumstances, and a reaffirmation of his convictions.

Finding such insights and benefits can make the querent feel better about his loss, as well as reveal tools or building blocks he can use in his next endeavor. Often, though, the types of things that the card in this position illustrates are intangible (such as Lincoln's commitment to his convictions), so it can take more than a surface reading of card 5 to bring them to light.

POSITION SIX: WHAT CAN YOU DO TO SET YOURSELF ON THE ROAD TO RECOVERY?
This position, which is the first in the Failure's Alchemy spread explicitly designed to advise specific actions, addresses the querent's recovery from his failure. This concern is more immediate than the strategic planning for his future success that is addressed in positions seven and nine since a still-damaged psyche will handicap the querent's efforts in his next venture. Full recovery before setting off on a new endeavor would be ideal, of course, but it is unrealistic to expect or demand that much, so this position assumes the more reasonable goal of just setting the querent on the road to recovery.

POSITION SEVEN: WHAT CAN YOU DO DIFFERENTLY NEXT TIME?

The question posed by this position seems so basic for this type of reading that one might wonder why it was not the first one asked in this spread. The reason it was placed at the end of this seven-card arc is that learning, healing, and picking up the pieces, which were covered by the prior six cards, are all necessary processes for the querent to undertake preparatory to moving on with his life. Now that those steps have been addressed, he is ready to talk about "next time." It follows, then, that it is helpful to interpret this card in light of what the previous cards had to say. Also, it is important to focus on improvement rather than on blame or negative criticism when interpreting this card. In other words, we should be sure to concentrate more on how the querent can improve his future performance than on his past mistakes.

POSITION EIGHT: WHERE ELSE IN YOUR LIFE CAN YOU FIND FULFILLMENT AT THIS TIME?

Since this position is not aimed at a discussion about either the querent's past defeat or his success in future endeavors, it may seem out of place in this spread. It is true that it diverts attention to other aspects of the querent's life, but rather than being an irrelevant tangent, this is actually a very therapeutic step in that it contributes to the querent's healing process.

Too often, when someone suffers a defeat, he lets that failure define him, or he becomes obsessed with redeeming himself through a future victory. At such times, he needs to gain some perspective on his life, and the message of the card in this position will provide that. It is intended to keep the querent from overly—and dysfunctionally—focusing on his failure by showing him that it does not, and should not, define his sense of who he is. As a result, this card can contribute to his sense of wholeness and help repair his sense of self-worth. Indirectly, this is a valuable step toward preparing the querent for his next venture.

POSITION NINE: WHERE CAN YOU GO FROM HERE, OR WHAT NEW VENTURE CAN YOU LOOK FORWARD TO?

After a defeat, some people become risk-averse, afraid to try again, while others veer to the opposite extreme and rush recklessly ahead in hopes that they can find redemption in a glorious victory. Consequently, the last card in this spread is intended to encourage a querent either to "get back up on the horse" or to reassess his goals rationally, depending on which extreme he is tending toward. So this card can provide the querent with hope and direction as it looks forward to see what opportunities await him.

Other Notes About This Spread

The first seven cards in the Failure's Alchemy spread can be viewed as an expanded Past, Present, Future spread. The first three cards look back at the querent's defeat in order to understand it and learn from it, while the fifth through seventh cards turn our attention toward the future to see how the querent can move away from his failure and toward new achievements. The card in the middle of this seven-card arc generally talks about the present—that is, where the querent can find help now. However, the present balances on the razor's edge between past and future, so interpreting this fourth card requires some flexibility. In the case of Lincoln's reading, the Tower (card 4) referred to the current state of affairs: the political storm raging over the issue of the abolition of slavery. In addition, though, it was about the catastrophic event that this political storm presaged—the Civil War—and so this card also referred to the future, a future that was inextricably being created by Lincoln's present.

Together, these seven cards can offer a unified story about where the querent came from, where he is now, and how he can pave the way toward a better future. Therefore, I like to summarize their message before completing the reading with the final two cards.

The layout of the Failure's Alchemy spread was designed to have a visual symmetry, but on a deeper level there is a logical symmetry to it as well. In Lincoln's reading, this resulted in the dualities evident in the summarization of the first seven cards. For example, we may compare cards 1 and 7, keeping in mind the fact that we only can change (card 7) what we take responsibility for (card 1). Thus, interpretation of the seventh card in this spread can be aided by considering the implications of the first card. Likewise, personal recovery often depends to a great extent on self-forgiveness, which implies a relationship between the second and sixth cards. Finally, there is a similarity of purpose in the third and fifth cards, which talk about learning from failure (card 3) and then salvaging something from it (card 5).

I find this deeper level of symmetry to be as appealing and satisfying as it is useful, and I wish I could take credit for consciously incorporating it into this spread's design. However, the fact is that it just turned out that way, as if of its own accord. Of course, this does not mean it was accidental, for perhaps a higher consciousness than my own guided my hand in creating this spread, as it may guide yours when you create your own spreads with an open mind and heart.

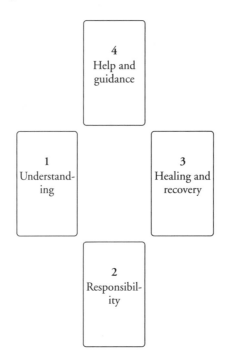

Figure 30. The Abbreviated Failure's Alchemy spread.

Alternative Spreads

An obvious subsidiary spread within the Failure's Alchemy spread consists of the first seven cards. Thus, we can create a somewhat smaller spread for quicker readings by eliminating the last two cards, leaving just the seven-card arch.

Another simplified version of this spread consists of four positions that address the bare essentials of learning, taking responsibility, healing, and finding help. This Abbreviated Failure's Alchemy spread is depicted in Figure 30, and its positional meanings are as follows:

1. What do you need to understand about your failure?

2. What about your failure should you accept responsibility for?

3. What can you do to recover from this setback?

4. Where can you find help and guidance?

One other alternative is to redefine the positional meanings of the original spread so that they pertain to a specific type of failure or to the particular defeat for which a reading is being requested. As an illustration of this possibility, the following positional definitions have been specifically adapted to suit a reading to help a querent recover from a failed relationship.

1. What about this breakup must you accept responsibility for?

2. What should you forgive yourself for?

3. What can you learn about yourself due to this experience?

4. What can help you deal with this breakup?

5. What can you salvage from this relationship?

6. What can you do to set yourself on the road to recovery?

7. What self-improvement will help make your next relationship a better one?

8. In what nonromantic relationships can you find fulfillment?

9. How can you find a new love?

THE TREE OF LIFE SPREAD
A Ten-Card Spread

As noted in chapter 1, a Tarot spread may be created based on a philosophical, esoteric, or spiritual system. One of the Western esoteric systems most often associated with the Tarot is the Qabalah, and there are several spreads in the Tarot lore that are based on the Qabalistic diagram called the *Tree of Life*.[30] However, I never found one that completely satisfied me, so I decided to create my own based on this ancient source of wisdom.

Information about this system that is pertinent to this section's spread may be gleaned from the following brief discussion of the ten nodes (called *sephiroth*) on the Tree of Life (see Figure 31 for a diagram of the Tree of Life). It is from the meanings attributed to these ten sephiroth that I created the spread for this section.[31]

1. **Kether (Crown).** Beginning, seed or source, creative potential, the will to create, the desire to grow and evolve, a sense of union with other people and with the universe.

2. **Chokhmah (Wisdom).** Activity, insight, creative energy, wisdom that initiates movement from potential to the manifest.

---

30. For explanations of the structure and meaning of the Tree of Life that are more detailed than is possible here, see the references in the recommended reading list at the back of this book.

31. There are twenty-two paths connecting the ten nodes, but their explanations are not relevant to this spread and therefore are beyond the scope of this discussion.

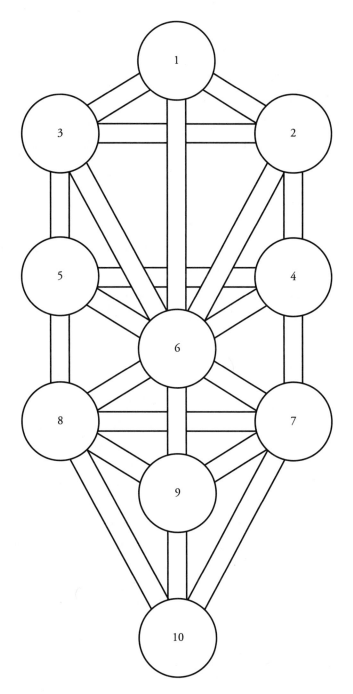

Figure 31. The Tree of Life.

3. **Binah (Understanding).** Receptivity, restriction, limitation, constraint, containment.

4. **Chesed (Mercy).** Unselfish giving, authority, vision, creativity in leadership, compassion and caring.

5. **Gevurah (Judgment/Strength).** Unselfish withholding, judgment and justice, severity, the warrior; preserving, upholding, and defending the status quo.

6. **Tiphereth (Beauty).** Harmony, integrity, balance, wholeness, self-sacrifice.

7. **Netzach (Victory).** Passion, pleasure, feelings, needs and drives, emotions, empathy, sympathy, intuition, dominance.

8. **Hod (Splendor/Glory).** Reason, abstraction, communication, conceptualization, logic, ownership, a sense of order, submission.

9. **Yesod (Foundation).** Imagination, the unconscious, instinct, illusion, dreams and creative visualization, hidden structure or agenda.

10. **Malkuth (Kingdom).** Mother Earth, the natural world, possessions, tangible results, practicality, stability, inertia.

This system is quite flexible in its scope and applicability, and the ten sephiroth can be interpreted as aspects of the divine or as states of consciousness (among other things). The spread in this section was created by considering them to be states of consciousness—that is, by using the Tree of Life as a model of human consciousness.

To create a spread based on this system, my first step was to model the spread's layout on the pattern of the Tree of Life diagram in Figure 31. Next, I considered the meanings of the ten sephiroth to discern various possible definitions for each of the ten positions of the spread. Then I chose one meaning per position with an eye toward creating a spread with a unified theme. This resulted in a spread that is useful in general readings about the querent's creativity and spiritual path or in more specific readings that can examine a proposed endeavor.

The Spread

Begin by dealing ten cards as indicated in Figure 32.

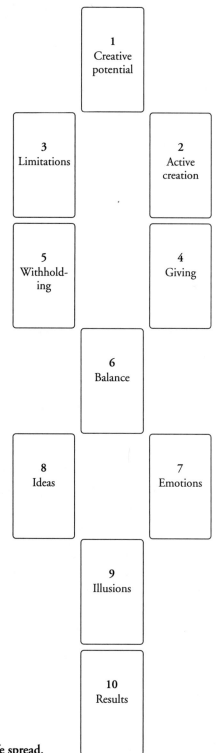

Figure 32. The Tree of Life spread.

193

Interpret these cards using the following positional meanings:

1. What do you have the potential to create in your life?

2. What are you actively creating now?

3. What boundaries or limitations do you need to set?

4. What should you give to others?

5. What should you hold on to for yourself?

6. How can you achieve harmony, balance, and wholeness in your endeavors?

7. Where are your emotions, passions, and desires leading you?

8. How are your beliefs, ideas, and concepts affecting how you see your current situation?

9. What illusions do you harbor about your life and the world around you?

10. What are the probable results of your endeavors?

A KnightHawk Reading with the Tree of Life Spread

Dear KnightHawk,

When my beloved father died recently, I ascended to the throne. Since then, I have tried to be a good ruler, but I find that the crown weighs heavily upon my brow, so I would like to have a Tarot reading to find out what the cards can tell me about my reign.

Specifically, I am curious about a bold idea I have. You see, although I am the queen of a great kingdom, the fame of another monarch, King Solomon of Israel, is intriguing, even to me. The wisdom and prosperity of this king are legendary, and I have considered traveling to Jerusalem to meet him so I can see for myself if all that I have heard about him is true. The journey would be long and difficult, but it might serve both my interests and those of my people, since Israel could prove to be an important ally as well as a valuable trading partner.

What can the cards tell me about this proposal and how it might affect my reign as queen?

With warm regards,
Her Majesty, the Queen of Sheba

*   *   *

Your Majesty,

It is an honor to do a reading to provide you with guidance about governing your kingdom. It seems that your main concern at this time is your question about traveling to Israel, so this reading focuses on that issue, although you also will find comments and advice about your rule in general since that is of concern to you as well.

The following are the cards that I have dealt for you.

1. What do you have the potential to create in your life?
   Eight of Cups

2. What are you actively creating now?
   Four of Wands

3. What boundaries or limitations do you need to set?
   King of Pentacles

4. What should you give to others?
   Nine of Wands reversed

5. What should you hold on to for yourself?
   Five of Cups reversed

6. How can you achieve harmony, balance, and wholeness in your endeavor?
   Queen of Pentacles reversed

7. Where are your emotions, passions, and desires leading you?
   The Tower reversed

8. How are your beliefs, ideas, and concepts affecting how you see your current situation?
   Ten of Wands reversed

9. What illusions do you harbor about your life and the world around you?
   Two of Wands reversed

10. What are the probable results of your endeavor?
    Six of Pentacles reversed

I will begin with a general note about these ten cards taken as a whole. The thing that stands out the most about them is the fact that the first three cards are upright, while the remaining seven are reversed. In order to explain what is remarkable about this, let me digress for a moment and tell you something about the philosophy behind this spread, which is called the Tree of Life spread.

The first three cards in this spread correspond to what is called the *supernal triangle*. These cards represent messages from your higher self or a higher source, and so they comment on your spiritual path. The remaining cards, which make up the lower portion of the Tree of Life, relate to the more mundane aspects of your being and how your life's purpose is being manifested. This description is, of course, a simplification of the concepts underlying the Tree of Life, but it is sufficient in order to make an important observation about your reading. This observation is that the orientation of the cards (reversed or upright) in this reading indicates that theoretically your proposal is a sound one with positive potential for your life's purpose. However, you should be careful in the execution of your plans, for the effort to bring them to fruition will be difficult and dangerous. This does not mean that you should abandon it or fear it, just that it requires careful planning and that you must exercise caution and vigilance during the journey itself, should you choose to undertake it.

Let us turn now to the individual cards. The first one, the Eight of Cups, indicates your disappointment or dissatisfaction with something, such as the way things are going in your kingdom or the course of your reign. It also shows you traveling somewhere to find new meaning and a new way of life—perhaps for yourself as well as for your people. So a new way of living and of governing is the primary potential of your life, and whether you realize it yet or not, it seems to be your primary motive for your plan to travel to Israel. And since this card shows you leaving behind old, familiar ways and past accomplishments in order to find a higher truth and a way that is more fulfilling, the implication is that this trip also has the potential to revitalize your life and enlighten your spiritual path. On a more mundane level, the Eight of Cups is considered to be one of the "travel cards" in the Tarot deck, which makes it an interesting, and auspicious, beginning for this reading.

The next card is the Four of Wands, which says that you are bringing stability, harmony, and prosperity to your people through your efforts to create a strong foundation for your kingdom's continued welfare and growth. Your proposal, then, should be evaluated in light of this message. Will a trip to meet King Solomon further your goals of building this strong foundation? This card is encouragement in that direction. On another note, this card also might indicate your kingdom's celebration of your ascent to the throne. This should be a time of joy and jubilation for you too. This presents an interesting contrast with the message of the previous card, thus making the longing for something new that is indicated there more poignant and maybe a bit perplexing to you. If so, realize that the dissatisfaction and yearning depicted in the Eight of Cups is a healthy sign of growth rather than one of ingratitude, ennui, or jadedness.

Moving on, we come to the King of Pentacles, a capable and dependable ruler who provides for the stability and prosperity of his subjects. As such, his message is that your future decisions and actions should be constrained by the fact that your primary responsibility is to provide for the safety and welfare of your people. Sometimes this may require you to put on a show of confidence when you feel disillusioned and of strength when you feel despair.

The next card, which indicates what you should give to others, is the reversed Nine of Wands. Generally, the Nine of Wands is about the strength of will and character that develops out of overcoming hardships, the wariness that develops as we prepare for renewed conflict, or the defensive boundaries we sometimes set up in anticipation of a resumed battle or strife. Since this card is reversed, though, I see it saying that you should endeavor to give your people secure borders, and at the same time, avoid wars so they can stop feeling defensive and wary. Your kingdom may be in a state of temporary peace right now, but a more permanent one would benefit your people greatly. Again, evaluate your proposed journey based on how well it will further this goal. Alternatively, though, we may consider the reversed Nine of Wands in light of the creative potential that was implied by the Eight of Cups. In that case, it may be saying that you can provide for the good of your people by working to break through or transcend the boundaries of the old ways of doing things.

Just as there are things you should give to others, there also are some things that you need to withhold from your people, which is discussed by the next card: the reversed Five of Cups. This card indicates dealing with and releasing your grief over the loss of your father so that you can move on with your life. This is something you need to do for yourself, even if it means that you must take some time out to do so. Perhaps as you do this, you can try to see the strength and authority that your father left you, and then hold on to that and make it your own. This card also advises you to keep your feelings of loss and sorrow private, possibly because they can discourage or dishearten your subjects.

Turning now to advice about achieving harmony, balance, and wholeness, we come to the reversed Queen of Pentacles in position six. Since this card is reversed, it indicates a need for you to develop the characteristics associated with this Queen: resourcefulness, practicality, generosity, and inner strength. Having been born into royalty, you have had your every personal need satisfied, so maybe you have not had a pressing need to develop resourcefulness and practicality before. However, these qualities will prove valuable if you do embark on your proposed journey. Also, this card's advice about generosity reinforces the message of the King of Pentacles about providing for the safety and welfare of your people.

Next, in the position that talks about where your emotions, passions, and desires are leading you, the reversed Tower card indicates that you have a passion for peaceful change within your kingdom, and it says that your desire to travel to Jerusalem may help your kingdom avoid a crisis or catastrophe. Perhaps this means that you will forge an alliance with Israel that will avert a future war. Or maybe you will find new ideas there that will lead you to institute gradual, evolutionary changes in your kingdom, which may diffuse pent-up energy that otherwise could lead to violent revolutionary change. In any case, this card is a good sign that your desired journey can help you provide your people with peace, security, and reform, which we previously saw recommended by the reversed Nine of Wands.

Moving on to the arena of your thoughts, beliefs, and views, the reversed Ten of Wands says that you seem to be daunted by the magnitude of your royal duties and responsibilities. Thus, you think that ruling your kingdom may be too burdensome and that you need to lighten the load a bit. By comparison, then, the long journey to Israel may appear to be less a burden than an opportunity to escape the responsibilities and obligations of the crown. Perhaps you also think of this trip as a means to see your way forward more clearly by getting out from under the burdens of state for a while.

In the position about the illusions you harbor, we find the Two of Wands card, which is about having a clear vision of where you are going and making bold plans to get there. Since this card is reversed, it says that your illusion may be the fear that a woman should not be so bold or visionary, or that as queen, you should not leave your kingdom for such a lengthy trip. In either case, this card advises you to trust yourself to make bold plans and to dare great deeds. Additionally, the reversed Two of Wands indicates that your vision of the world may be too limited or parochial, so it advises you to widen your horizons. It does seem that your proposed journey, which will take you to exotic lands and expose you to new experiences, promises to do just that.

We come now to the last card in this spread, the reversed Six of Pentacles, which describes the probable outcome of a trip to Israel to meet its king. First, it depicts King Solomon sharing his knowledge and wisdom with you. However, the reversal of this card predicts that contrary to your expectations, this sharing of concepts and ideas may go in both directions, so remember that you bring your own wisdom with you. Similarly, this card seems to be a warning not to let yourself be placed in the untenable position of being a supplicant to King Solomon. Approach him as an equal, for failure to do so can result in difficulties in achieving balanced trade and diplomatic relations with Israel.

A very different message in the reversed Six of Pentacles is one that concerns the probable effect of this venture on your people and on your relationship with them. Consider that this card's image in its reversed orientation places the poor people in it above the wealthy nobleman. The implication here is that the wisdom and experience you can gain from your journey will help you improve the condition of your people and lessen the social distance that separates them from you. This result would be in accord with the admonition of the King of Pentacles to provide for the welfare of your people. It also may be a manifestation of the message of the Four of Wands about contributing to the stability of your kingdom, and it reflects the new way of living and ruling that the Eight of Cups said you have the potential to manifest.

Now let's turn to a few clusters of cards within this spread to see what messages we can find there. First, consider cards 1, 2, and 3—the supernal triangle that I mentioned previously. Taken together, these three cards say that your kingdom is doing well at this time as it celebrates its new queen's ascension to the throne (Four of Wands). You, however, have a sense of dissatisfaction, a feeling that there is something more important yet to find, which has impelled you to consider a journey to foreign lands (Eight of Cups). If you undertake such a quest, be sure to keep in mind that your primary responsibility is to provide for the welfare of your people (King of Pentacles). In other words, be sure that you don't let your sense of dissatisfaction turn you away from your primary duties of being queen, for that would lead you away from the true path of your soul.

The next cluster consists of the three cards running down the right side of the spread: cards 2, 4, and 7. This column relates to mercy and giving, and the common theme running through its cards is one of safety and protection. Consequently, I see that these are things for you to create for your kingdom and to give to your people. So if we read these three cards as one sentence, so to speak, they say that you are striving to create a safe space and a secure foundation for your people (Four of Wands) that will provide them with protection from further conflicts (Nine of Wands reversed) and lead them away from future crises and catastrophes (the Tower reversed).

The three cards running down the other side of this spread—cards 3, 5, and 8—deal with severity and constraints in your life and in the world around you. The King of Pentacles indicates your responsibility to provide for the needs of your people while the reversed Ten of Wands depicts your concern that you may not be able to carry the burden of that responsibility. To bridge the gap between this requirement and your ability to fulfill it, the reversed Five of Cups suggests that you seek strength and guidance from the memory and spirit of your deceased father. Also, once you have finished mourning his death, you will know that he is still with you in spirit and that you have inherited from him the power and courage to bear the responsibilities of your office.

Another obvious cluster of cards is the middle column—cards 1, 6, 9, and 10—which is concerned with balancing the giving quality of the cards on the right with the constraints of the cards on the left. These four cards say that you can leave behind and transcend (Eight of Cups) your parochial view of the world (reversed Two of Wands) in order to find a new vision for serving the needs of your people (reversed Six of Pentacles), but to do so requires inner strength and resourcefulness (reversed Queen of Pentacles). Thus, the qualities that the Queen of Pentacles recommends will enable you to balance your desire to provide for the safety and welfare of your people (the right-hand column) with your worries and fears that this responsibility may be too great for you (the left-hand column).

Cards 4 and 5 (Nine of Wands reversed and Five of Cups reversed) discuss giving versus withholding, and they form an interesting pair due to their common theme of past loss and pain. They say that in order to give your people security and protection from strife and conflict, you first must do something for yourself: you must find healing from your own personal loss and experience the growth that comes from such healing.

Two other cards that present an illuminating message are cards 7 and 8—emotions and desires versus thoughts and beliefs. The reversed Tower says that at a gut level, you see that fundamental changes are necessary in your kingdom if it is to avoid a crisis. However, the reversed Ten of Wands shows how the day-to-day burdens of the affairs of state keep you from seeing the way to plan such changes, so perhaps getting away from them for a time will help you do so. Thus, this implies a recommendation regarding your proposed trip to Israel.

Finally, let me conclude with a summary of the most important points of this reading. The primary theme here—which the first card, the Eight of Cups, illustrated—is your quest to find a new and more fulfilling way of life for yourself and for your people. The venture you propose has the potential to do this, for it is a sound one, but you need to plan and prepare for it carefully, and you must undertake it with caution and resourcefulness. Meanwhile, you feel overwhelmed by the royal responsibilities that you carry, and it is tempting to see this journey as a way to escape that burden rather than as a means to learn how to bear it and how to see your way forward despite it. A trip to Israel to meet King Solomon may help you do that, but only if you also can overcome your sense of loss due to your father's death and thereby cultivate your own inner strength so you can approach the king of Israel as an equal. Also, if you do choose to take this course of action, keep in mind that your primary responsibility is to provide for the security and welfare of your kingdom.

Thank you for requesting this reading, Your Majesty. I hope it helps you.

Best of luck,
KnightHawk

Comments on a Reading with the Tree of Life Spread

Although the Queen of Sheba is mentioned in Judaic and Islamic lore, as well as in Ethiopian legend, today we know little about her. Indeed, we lack conclusive evidence as to whether she was fictional or real, but this did not seem to be an obstacle to doing a reading for her since I have done KnightHawk readings in either case. More troubling was the fact that the disparate sources that mention her provide conflicting tales, which may lend mystery and mystique to her name, but it also leads to confusion and uncertainty about her life.

In order to do this section's reading, then, I relied upon the biblical tale of this queen's visit to the court of King Solomon (1 Kings:10), which eliminated the discrepancies that arise from conflicting stories. However, even using just one account, I found my task complicated by the fact that the brevity of the biblical tale left me with important pieces of the Queen of Sheba's background untold. This compelled me to make a few logical inferences about her as I prepared to do this reading.

Perhaps the most significant question left unanswered is why she traveled to Jerusalem to visit King Solomon. Such a journey would have been atypical for a queen of that time, being long, difficult, and dangerous. I doubt that it was merely curiosity that motivated her, although that may have played a part in her decision. It is more probable that her reasons were based on matters of trade or politics, as we saw in this reading. For example, both the reversed Nine of Wands (card 4) and the reversed Tower (card 7) implied that one motive was to avoid a repetition of past conflicts and wars, which was supported by her concern for the welfare of her people, as indicated by the King of Pentacles (card 3).

To create the question for this reading, I had to make some assumptions as to why this queen would have made such a perilous journey, but I tried to leave as many options open as I could in order to avoid biasing the reading. Also, as I drafted the question for this reading, it grew to be rather complex. This was not surprising since the Queen of Sheba's situation undoubtedly was more complicated than that of someone who just wanted to take a vacation. In fact, it seemed there should be several issues implicit in the Queen of Sheba's question, ranging from a general concern about how her reign would fare to specific ones about the advisability and probable outcome of a trip to Jerusalem.

Fortunately, the complexity of this question offered an opportunity to demonstrate how one can deal with multifaceted questions, which are rather common. There are many ways of managing such situations, and finding and focusing on the main issue, as demonstrated in the reading for the Queen of Sheba, is one of them. Other options include doing separate readings for each subsidiary question or creating a spread in which each position addresses one specific subquestion.

Also, this multilayered question worked well with the Tree of Life spread since it is designed to cover a topic from many different perspectives and on many different levels. However, in order to provide some focus for the reading, I did choose one main area to concentrate on, although by keeping in mind all that the querent had asked, I was able to address her ancillary issues to some extent as well.

Specific Notes About Individual Positions in the Spread

POSITION ONE: WHAT DO YOU HAVE THE POTENTIAL TO CREATE IN YOUR LIFE?

The first card in the Tree of Life spread generally sets the tone and basic theme for the reading, and so it also influences how each of the subsequent cards will be interpreted. In fact, the message of card 1 is reflected often throughout a reading with this spread. In the reading for the Queen of Sheba, for example, we saw the Eight of Cups's message of leaving behind the old in order to search for something new and better echoed often, especially in the interpretation of cards 2 (Four of Wands), 4 (Nine of Wands reversed), and 7 (the Tower reversed).

POSITION TWO: WHAT ARE YOU ACTIVELY CREATING NOW?

For general readings using this spread, the card in position two can be interpreted as an indication of how the querent is currently manifesting her creative potential. However, if the question for the reading deals with a proposed endeavor, as was the case in the reading for the Queen of Sheba, this card can discuss considerations that the querent should keep in mind as she evaluates that proposal.

In addition, a comparison between this card and the first one can provide further insights into the meanings of one or both of them. In this section's reading, that comparison was discussed during the examination of card 2, but we also might consider cards 1 and 2 as a two-card spread and discuss their joint interpretation later in the reading when we are examining the other subspreads.

POSITION THREE: WHAT BOUNDARIES OR LIMITATIONS DO YOU NEED TO SET?

A common mistake in using this spread is to see the limits and constraints on the querent's actions that are depicted in card 3 as being problems or negative influences. Sometimes they may be, but boundary definitions can be quite helpful since we all need to know our limitations, and we can focus our efforts better when we have limited and defined the scope of our actions or endeavors.

POSITION FOUR: WHAT SHOULD YOU GIVE TO OTHERS?

The message of the card in position four can be both a concrete example of what card 2 said the querent is actively creating and advice about effective ways for her to manifest that creativity. Thus, our interpretation of the fourth card in this spread is aided by keeping in mind the meaning of card 2. In this section's reading, for example, the message of the reversed Nine of Wands reflected the themes of stability, prosperity, and growth that were apparent in the Four of Wands.

Additionally, it is important to point out that although card 4 is about giving, it is not about giving something away. In other words, this card is more about generosity than about sacrifice. It depicts what the querent can give to others, which is a course of action that ultimately will help her as much as it will benefit them. These are useful considerations to keep in mind when reading this card, especially if the querent is resistant to hearing its message, perhaps fearing that it is asking her to suffer a loss.

POSITION FIVE: WHAT SHOULD YOU HOLD ON TO FOR YOURSELF?

The fifth card in this spread is like the flip side of card 4. Instead of what the querent should give, it is about what she should withhold, or refrain from giving. Again, it is easy to misinterpret the intent of this position. It is not about selfishly grasping on to something. Rather, it is concerned with the necessity of holding something back or keeping something for oneself—not out of greed, but out of concern for the benefit of all. For example, a parent might keep his child from eating candy in order to protect his or her health, or a teacher might avoid confusing her students with more information than they can handle.

Also, like card 4, the fifth card is closely related to the card above it, so it is useful to consider card 3 when interpreting card 5. In this section's reading, the cause of the querent's grief and mourning, depicted in the Five of Cups, was seen to be the death of her father, the king, partly because of the close proximity of the King of Pentacles.

POSITION SIX: HOW CAN YOU ACHIEVE HARMONY, BALANCE, AND WHOLENESS IN YOUR ENDEAVOR?

Just as card 1 sets the tone for a reading with the Tree of Life spread, card 6 can be the pivotal point that brings it into balance. While the cards on the right-hand side of the spread are associated with giving and creating and those on the left with withholding and constraints, the advice of card 6 generally helps the querent balance these two extremes. Consequently, its advice is of great importance for a reading with this spread, and sometimes we can use it to help the querent bridge the gap or resolve apparent contrasts between cards 2 and 3, between cards 4 and 5, and between cards 7 and 8.

POSITION SEVEN: WHERE ARE YOUR EMOTIONS, PASSIONS, AND DESIRES LEADING YOU?
Although at first glance position seven appears to be one of prediction—and certainly, the message of the card in this position may be somewhat prophetic—its main purpose is to show the querent how the course of her life is being affected by emotions and desires of which she may not be consciously aware. As a result, she may (or may not) want to adjust her path to conform more to her rational ideas of where her life should be going. As for this card's predictive qualities, it is an indication of the direction in which the querent's passion is leading her rather than of what fate has in store for her.

POSITION EIGHT: HOW ARE YOUR BELIEFS, IDEAS, AND CONCEPTS AFFECTING HOW YOU SEE YOUR CURRENT SITUATION?
There are two different, but complementary, ways of working with the card in position eight. First, this card can discuss the querent's beliefs in general. This may seem unnecessary, since we might assume that she already knows what she believes. In reality, though, the message revealed here sometimes comes as a surprise to the querent. At the very least, the dialogue that this card may initiate can help the querent through the valuable process of articulating and analyzing her basic values and assumptions as they relate to the issue at hand.

Secondly, card 8 can show the querent how she sees her current situation. Since her view of it may involve anything from a flawed analysis to a cogent insight, this way of interpreting this card can open up a dialogue that will help the querent think about her situation more clearly.

Although we can use either one of these methods individually, usually they can be combined in order to show the querent how her beliefs are influencing her view of the situation addressed by this reading. For example, in the Queen of Sheba's reading, the reversed Ten of Wands said that the querent believed that the role of being queen was too burdensome, which led her to see a perilous journey to Israel as being easy by comparison.

POSITION NINE: WHAT ILLUSIONS DO YOU HARBOR ABOUT YOUR LIFE AND THE WORLD AROUND YOU?
The illusions that card 9 may describe can range from a misguided point of view to a benign view through rose-tinted glasses. Although some illusions are dysfunctional, we must be careful not to judge all of them as being negative. Since our expectations contribute to the creation of our reality—or to our enjoyment and appreciation of it—there can be value in seeing something that does not exist—at least, not yet. Even when the

querent's illusions are counterproductive, we still may find advice in card 9 about coping with those illusions. We might try to see what the reality beneath the illusion is, how the querent can overcome her illusion, or what benefit she might extract from it.

POSITION TEN: WHAT ARE THE PROBABLE RESULTS OF YOUR ENDEAVOR?

Position ten completes this spread, and the card in this position illustrates the final result of the querent's situation or proposal. If the reading is a general one, card 10 indicates where her life is headed generally. If, on the other hand, the reading is about a specific endeavor, card 10 describes its probable outcome. In either case, though, if the querent does not like what she sees, she may choose to adjust her decisions and actions in order to alter the course of her life, and the information presented by the prior nine cards should help her do so.

In addition to completing a reading with the Tree of Life spread, card 10 also can bring it full circle if we try to see how it relates to the querent's potential, as indicated in card 1. In fact, in the reading for the Queen of Sheba, I was able to reflect the message of card 10 back to each of the first three cards in the spread.

Other Notes About This Spread

As with most spreads having more than a few cards, the Tree of Life spread has embedded within it several significant subspreads whose individual interpretations can contribute to the overall message of the reading. There are many such subspreads in the Tree of Life spread, several of which were illustrated in this section's reading.

The most obvious place to find ideas for significant card clusters in this particular spread is in the underlying structure of the Qabalistic Tree of Life itself. The first three nodes in the Tree of Life are called the supernal triangle, and if we consider this diagram to be a model of human consciousness, then these nodes correspond to a person's super-ego, conscience, or higher self. Considered from a theological point of view, these three nodes can be thought of as our connection to the divine or our soulful purpose. In the reading for the Queen of Sheba, the subspread consisting of cards 1, 2, and 3 provided a view of the querent's life from a higher (i.e., nonegocentric) viewpoint, as they related her life's purpose (to provide for the welfare of her people) to her spiritual yearning for something more in her life.

Next, we can consider the three columns in this diagram. The nodes on the right—nodes two, four, and seven—form what is known as the *Pillar of Mercy* and are associated with giving and expansion. This section's reading saw in the three corresponding cards a common theme, which gave the Queen of Sheba a general directive for what she should give to her people.

On the left, nodes three, five, and eight comprise the *Pillar of Severity,* which traditionally represents withholding and constraints. As opposed to the three cards in the right-hand column, this three-card subspread in the reading for the Queen of Sheba did not present an obvious common theme. Instead, each card approached the issue of constraints in a different way so that when combined, they not only suggested how the querent's actions were constrained, but also what her resistance to operating within that constraint was and how to overcome that resistance.

The middle pillar—nodes one, six, nine, and ten—represents a balance between the extremes of the other two pillars. For the Queen of Sheba, the basic meanings of these four cards were assembled into one cohesive message. Then, in light of that message, advice for balancing the opposing energies of the left and right pillars was found in the reading's central card: card 6 (the reversed Queen of Pentacles).

There are a few dualistic pairs of cards in the Tree of Life spread that form valuable two-card subspreads. These pairs arise naturally from a comparison of the right and left columns in the tree. Card 4 (giving to others) and card 5 (withholding for yourself) form an interesting pair due to their contrasting definitions and the irony that often results from their similarities. For example, the Queen of Sheba discovered that in order to heal the wounds of her people, she needed to heal her own wounds first.

Card 7 (emotions and desires) and card 8 (thought and reason) present two complementary ways of perceiving and dealing with reality. Quite often, what the querent feels about a situation and what she thinks about it are two entirely different things, and this discrepancy can set up a host of internal conflicts within her. Seeing and understanding this discrepancy, however, can set the querent on the road to resolving it. In this section's reading, for example, these two cards addressed the querent's conflict between her desire for peaceful change and her problems understanding how to act upon and actualize that desire.

Finally, card 2 discusses what the querent is creating, while card 3 indicates constraints on that effort. These two cards form a subspread that I did not use explicitly in the reading for the Queen of Sheba because I had interpreted each of these two cards in light of the other earlier in the reading. Keep in mind, then, that each of these subspreads is a tool that we can use when they prove beneficial. Although generally it is a good idea to consider them, we need only employ them when they contribute to the sense and meaning of a reading.

Alternative Spreads

Since each of the ten nodes or sephiroth on the Tree of Life encompasses a wide range of meaning, obvious alternative spreads are the ones that you can create out of your own understanding of their concepts—either based on the descriptions presented earlier in this section or on your own studies of the subject. Thus, the Qabalistic Tree of Life can inspire a variety of spreads using the card layout in Figure 32, but with new positional meanings that suit your particular needs. For example, the following is another Tree of Life spread, but this one is intended specifically for relationship readings.

1. In what ways do you feel a sense of union with your romantic partner?

2. What wisdom about your relationship should you be acting upon?

3. What understanding about your relationship do you need to be receptive to?

4. How are you providing leadership in this relationship?

5. How are you judging your partner?

6. What do you need to sacrifice in order to find balance in your relationship?

7. How are you trying to dominate your partner?

8. In what ways are you being submissive in this relationship?

9. How are your dreams and imagination shaping your relationship?

10. Where in this relationship do you need to apply more self-discipline?

The two Western esoteric systems most often associated with the Tarot are the Qabalah and astrology. This section's Tree of Life spread was inspired by the former, and there are many spreads in the Tarot literature inspired by the latter. However, anyone with a decent understanding of astrology can create his or her own astrological Tarot spread. A circular shape for such a spread should work well, with twelve card positions placed around it like the hours on a clock.

The following is an example of how we might define these twelve positions based on the twelve astrological signs. The intention of this particular Astrological spread is to help the querent improve herself by seeking to develop some of the best characteristics of each astrological sign.

1. (Aries) How can you become more independent and self-confident?

2. (Taurus) Where in your life do you need to exercise more patience and practicality?

3. (Gemini) How can you cultivate friendliness and congeniality in your life?

4. (Cancer) How can you best express your devotion to your loved ones?

5. (Leo) What part of your life should you be more enthusiastic about?

6. (Virgo) How can industry and practicality help you accomplish your goals?

7. (Libra) What can bring more harmony and balance into your life?

8. (Scorpio) Where can determination and willpower take you?

9. (Sagittarius) What can help you become more cheerful and gregarious?

10. (Capricorn) Where in your life do you need to apply more self-discipline and ambition?

11. (Aquarius) What unconventional idea or cause would you do well to pursue?

12. (Pisces) For whom should you show more compassion and sympathy?

The above is, of course, just one possible Astrological spread. If you feel comfortable enough with astrology to create your own spread, try your hand at it. Since the result will be something into which you have invested a part of yourself, it should serve you quite well.

THE VARIABLE TIMING SPREAD

Timing questions of the form, "When is such-and-such going to happen?" are common, but in my experience, the Tarot does not work well as a clock or a calendar. Also, I do not like the implications of determinism inherent in using a Tarot reading that way.[32] However, not wishing to ignore such questions, I sought a timing spread that was nondeterministic, and eventually I found one (a spread suggested by former president of the American Tarot Association John Gilbert) that came close to suiting my needs. That spread was dynamic in that there were not a predetermined number of cards in it, and I liked how it used the cards to indicate milestones leading up to the questioned event rather than to count the days (or weeks, or months, etc.) preceding it. However, I wanted to allow the cards to give advice as well, based on the consideration that the querent has free will, so I created a new timing spread, which, like John Gilbert's, is dynamic and nondeterministic.

The resulting spread, the Variable Timing spread, is described in this section. I designed it for readings wherein the querent wonders when (or even if) some event or desired outcome will occur. It is intended to indicate milestones that will mark the journey toward that event and advice about how the querent may accelerate or facilitate his or her progress toward it. In addition, though, this spread also may indicate that it is improbable that the event in question will occur at all.

---

32. Although this describes how I use the Tarot, there are those who disagree. If you do want to use Tarot readings to provide such exact timing estimates, see the suggestions under the heading of "Alternative Spreads" at the end of this section.

The Spread

This spread does not use a proscribed number of cards or a set layout pattern. Rather, it employs an intuitive methodology. You may lay the cards out in a straight line, or whatever pattern works for you, but you must remember the order in which they were dealt.

To begin, slowly deal one card after another, face up, until one comes up that addresses the desired outcome. Of course, deciding when you have come to this outcome card is an intuitive call, but generally it is fairly obvious when it is dealt.

The cards dealt prior to the outcome card (the "prior-event cards") depict the sequence of events that have to happen before the final outcome occurs, and they indicate things that the querent needs to do or signs she should watch out for. Read these prior-event cards first, then interpret the outcome card, which may add insights into the nature of the desired outcome or it may indicate that it seems unlikely. If the very first card seems to depict the outcome, which means that there are no prior-event cards, then the outcome is either already at hand or quite imminent.

For example, consider a question like, "When will John and I get back together?" If, after a few prior-event cards, we get a card like the Lovers, Two of Cups, or Four of Wands, we may see this as an encouraging sign that the querent will get back together with her boyfriend. If, on the other hand, a card like the Hermit, Five of Cups, or Three of Swords comes up, we might see disappointment coming instead. Why would a card like the Hermit, Five of Cups, or Three of Swords be the outcome card and not a prior-event card? Actually, any one of those cards could be a prior-event card, but our intuition may tell us that it is the probable outcome instead.

Finally, if we deal quite a few cards and still do not get an outcome card, this may indicate that the desired outcome is either unlikely or too far in the future to predict at this time. How many cards constitute "quite a few" is another intuitive call for us to make in the course of the reading, but generally I limit this spread to fewer than ten cards.

A KnightHawk Reading with the Variable Timing Spread

Dear KnightHawk,

Twenty years ago, my husband, Odysseus, set sail to make war on Troy, and he has not yet returned. Dozens of suitors who, unlike me, assume that my husband is dead have descended upon my home, demanding that I choose one of them to wed. So far, I

have managed to avoid making this horrible choice, as I maintain hope of my husband's return. But with the passage of time, pressure from these suitors has grown ever stronger.

Meanwhile, my son recently returned from a search for his father with news that Odysseus is alive. So I would like to know, when will he come home to me and reclaim his rightful place as king of Ithaca?

Most sincerely yours,
Queen Penelope

*　*　*

My dear queen,

I am honored that you have sought my counsel at this troubled time in your life. Although I cannot use the Tarot to give you a precise date and time in answer to your question, I can do a reading to see what events or portents will precede your husband's return to the throne of Ithaca. Thus, this reading will help you recognize the signs that will herald his homecoming.

The cards I have dealt for you are as follows:

1. Strength

2. Seven of Cups

3. Two of Wands reversed

4. Knight of Swords

5. Knight of Wands

6. The Chariot

First of all, the power indicated by the Strength card is often subtle, hidden, or internal, so this card is an indication of things like courage and fortitude. Thus, one thing that I see in this card is that there already is great strength in your midst, even if you cannot see it yet. Actually, since a lion, like the one depicted on this card, can represent a king, I considered stopping here and saying that Odysseus is already home, but this did not seem to make sense. Surely, you would know if he were there, right? So I delved further into this card to see what else it may have to say. Considering the image on it, I saw that the great strength and power (represented by the lion) that is in your midst is friendly to you (represented by the woman embracing the lion), so this card is a good sign. In addition, it also offers the advice that you should maintain your own courage and fortitude, and not give in to despair.

The Seven of Cups comes next, and it is a card of illusions and dreams. For you, this may indicate the need to see through an illusion. Combining this insight with the advice of the previous card, I see that you will need to rely on your faith and courage in order to overcome an illusion wherein your emotions may cloud your perceptions. Also, due to its proximity to the reversed Two of Wands (the next card in this spread), I can see the Seven of Cups as an indication of wishful thinking, probably on the part of the suitors who beset you. In that case, this card is telling you to watch for a sign that their delusions have completely overcome them.

Next, the Two of Wands is often about dominion, but here it is reversed. Therefore, I see it saying that once these suitors are completely overcome by dreams of success and grandeur, as indicated by the previous card, they will have a false sense of dominion over you, and each will see himself as being close to gaining control over Ithaca. This card also advises you to feed that false sense of dominion, for it is indeed false, and it will presage their downfall.

At this point, I want to pause for a moment to present a general impression about the cards in this spread. In the first three cards, there is a sense of waiting and pensiveness, of action pending, but as yet postponed. But as we now proceed to the next three cards in this spread, there is an abrupt change of tempo. Suddenly, there is a sense of action, both swift and powerful.

There is a unity of focus and purpose in the next two cards, the two Knights. Knights signify action—especially the Knights of Swords and Wands—and these two are charging, weapons drawn, toward the reversed Two of Wands, which represents the false sense of dominion of your suitors. More specifically, I see in the

Knight of Swords an indication of your son manifesting a burgeoning sense of authority in the face of these suitors, as he is backed by the courage, confidence, and forcefulness of the Knight of Wands, which may represent your husband since we are almost at the end of this spread. Additionally, the Knight of Wands indicates a bold action that will follow quickly on the heels of your son's display of authority.

The final card, the Chariot, indicates victory, and in this reading, it appears to depict a triumphant return. This card is very encouraging, for not only does it predict the return of your husband, but it anticipates his conquest of your suitors as well.

In summary, I see in these cards encouragement for you to be brave, since the time for waiting should be over soon. Also, be watchful for the signs of action to come, and have faith that Odysseus will have the strength, power, and will to prevail.

Thank you for requesting this reading, Queen Penelope. I hope it helps you.

Best of luck,
KnightHawk

Comments on a Reading with the Variable Timing Spread

I chose to do this reading as if Penelope had sought KnightHawk's advice at the beginning of book 20 of *The Odyssey*. At that time, Odysseus had returned to Ithaca, but he was disguised as a beggar so that he could evaluate the situation there before taking action to rout the suitors who had infested his home. Although Penelope had met and befriended this beggar, she had failed to recognize him for who he was. Meanwhile, her suitors, equally ignorant of the beggar's true identity, had mocked and tormented him, their bloated arrogance having blinded them to the common courtesy of hospitality to strangers in need.

Odysseus did reveal himself to his son, Telemachus, who stood up to the suitors, confronting them with a litany of their vices, shortcomings, and misdeeds, and the next day, he and Odysseus attacked and defeated them. It was only then, after Odysseus had rid himself of these parasites, that he finally revealed himself to his wife, who had a hard time believing that he was really home at last.

This reading indicates that there were three essential factors in Odysseus's victory over Penelope's suitors. First, cards 2 and 3 say that the suitors' corruption and arrogance contributed to their own downfall. Card 4 indicates the importance of Telemachus's maturation and growing sense of his own power and authority, while cards 1 and 5 stress the obvious value of Odysseus's strength, courage, and forcefulness. While I had realized the importance of the first and third factors, the commensurate value of Telemachus's contribution was an interesting revelation.

Notes About This Spread

The reading for Penelope illustrates several important points about the use of the Variable Timing spread. First of all, while the prior-event cards may indicate either a milestone or a piece of advice, I try to see both aspects in them. For example, in this reading, the Strength card indicated that a powerful force was already at hand, and it also advised Penelope to maintain her courage.

Next, while interpreting the cards individually yields valuable insights, a message also may be found by viewing the spread as a whole in order to get an overall sense of the themes, tone, and flow of the reading. In this section's reading, the feel of the first three cards was contrasted with that of the final three cards, which indicated an "abrupt change of tempo" halfway through the spread. The change that it foresaw—when a feeling of tentativeness and stasis would give way to one of decision and action—would have been a major signpost for the querent in itself.

Finally, the hardest part of using this spread may be its requirement that we be able to know when we have reached the outcome card. The reading for Penelope illustrates this challenge in that I had to make an intuitive call regarding the first card, Strength, which could have been seen as an indication of Odysseus's return. Indeed, since he had returned to Ithaca at the time that this reading would have taken place, this could have been a valid place to stop, but it just felt right to keep going.

While this was an intuitive decision, I also was influenced by the fact that Penelope's question was ". . . when will he come home to me and reclaim his rightful place as king of Ithaca?" It was the phrase "and reclaim his rightful place as king of Ithaca" that demanded more from this reading. As it turned out, dealing several more cards, which each provided helpful advice, resulted in a better reading than would have been the case if I had stopped with the Strength card. Also, the card with which I did end this reading, the Chariot, seemed to be a much clearer outcome card.

Alternative Timing Spreads

As noted at the beginning of this section, when asked a timing question, I avoid doing a reading designed to give an answer in precise dates or time intervals. I prefer to handle such questions by rephrasing them to be something like, "What do you need to do to make this event happen?" However, sometimes I use a spread like the one presented in this section, which focuses on the sequence of events and requirements that must precede the outcome in question. Still, some Tarot readers are inclined to try to divine more explicit timing information, and for their sake, I have presented here several common methods for doing so.

One technique relies on the fact that both the Tarot suits and the seasons of the year have elemental correspondences, which relate the four suits to the four seasons. There are, of course, various correspondences of this sort, but the set of associations that I have found to be most common is the following:

Suit	Element	Season
Pentacles	Earth	Winter
Swords	Air	Autumn
Cups	Water	Spring
Wands	Fire	Summer

A common way to answer a timing question using these associations is to deal one card. One alternative is to use only the cards from the minor arcana, in which case the card's suit indicates the season of the event within the next twelve months. In that case, you may narrow the seasonal time frame further by considering the number on the minor arcana card to indicate the week within the season. Since there are thirteen weeks in a season, Pages can represent week eleven, Knights twelve, and Queens thirteen. The Kings, then, may indicate that the event can occur at any time within the season, but that the querent must take charge in order to make it happen.[33] As an example, consider doing a reading in which the card pulled is the Page of Wands. This would say that the event will occur in the eleventh week of the coming summer.[34]

---

33. A similar, but slightly different, scheme is described by Gail Fairfield in her book *Choice-Centered Tarot* (138–39).

34. If we consider that the first week of a season begins on the Sunday after the equinox, the dates for this eleventh week will be slightly different each year, but it will fall near the beginning of September.

If you decide to use the major arcana cards too, you may use the astrological sign associated with them to determine the timing of the event. Thus, for example, the Emperor, which is associated with Aries, would indicate the time frame of March 21 to April 20. To do so, you can use one of the most common sets of astrological associations, that of the Order of the Golden Dawn, which is depicted in Table 1. Note that ten major arcana cards are associated with a planet, the sun, or the moon, which indirectly associates them with a sign. However, this creates some ambiguity for the Magician and the Empress, which you may resolve in whatever way makes most sense to you.

Note that there are other elemental, seasonal, and astrological association schemes. If you prefer one that differs from what has been presented here, feel free to use it instead.

Yet another technique involves counting cards until you reach a specified type, in which case the number of cards turned over will indicate the number of days, weeks, months, or years until the questioned event will occur. To do this, first decide what time interval you will use: days, weeks, months, or years. Next, decide what type of card to use for a "stop" card. (It is most common to use either an Ace or a major arcana card.) Shuffle the cards, and then turn over one card at a time until you reach a stop card. The number of cards turned over prior to the stop card will tell you how many days (or weeks, months, or years, depending on what interval you have chosen to use) until the event will happen. If the first card you turn over is a stop card, this will indicate that the event is imminent. You also may use the orientation of the stop card (reversed or not) to indicate whether or not the questioned event is likely to occur.

In another method, you pick an interval in which an event might reasonably be expected to happen (such as seven days, four weeks, twelve months, four quarters, ten years, etc.) and then deal several cards, one for each unit of measure. For example, you might choose to deal seven cards, one per day of the coming week. Then the most encouraging card of those dealt, or the card that seems to represent the event best (for example, the Two of Cups for a wedding), will indicate the day (or week, month, quarter, or year) when the event will occur. If, however, there are no encouraging cards, then the event probably won't happen within the selected time frame.

Finally, there is an important consideration to keep in mind when doing a timing reading to seek precise dates or time intervals. Regardless of the technique you choose, it is vital that you decide on a system and impress it on your subconscious or communicate it to the universe prior to doing your reading. Then be sure to stick to that intention as you do the reading.

Major Arcana Card	Astrological Association
Fool	Uranus (rules Aquarius)
Magician	Mercury (rules Gemini and Virgo)
High Priestess	Moon (rules Cancer)
Empress	Venus (rules Taurus and Libra)
Emperor	Aries
Hierophant	Taurus
Lovers	Gemini
Chariot	Cancer
Strength	Leo
Hermit	Virgo
Wheel of Fortune	Jupiter (rules Sagittarius)
Justice	Libra
Hanged Man	Neptune (rules Pisces)
Death	Scorpio
Temperance	Sagittarius
Devil	Capricorn
Tower	Mars (rules Aries)
Star	Aquarius
Moon	Pisces
Sun	The sun (rules Leo)
Judgement	Pluto (rules Scorpio)
World	Saturn (rules Capricorn)

Table 1. Major arcana/astrological associations.

Alternative Nonspreads

Typically, a spread has a predefined layout or pattern into which an exact number of cards are dealt. Each of these cards is then interpreted based on the specified meaning for its position in the layout. However, this is not the only way to do a Tarot reading. The cards may be used in a looser way wherein the layout is not predefined or there are no set positional meanings. The method used for this section's reading is one such technique, but there are other ways of reading the cards without a spread as we traditionally think of it, and the following are a few additional examples.

The simplest Tarot reading involves using just one card in order to answer the querent's question. This card is read solely in light of the question asked, without a positional definition to add a context in which it should be interpreted. In fact, the querent's question itself assumes the role of the positional definition. This technique provides a quick reading and works well for relatively simple questions.

For more complex issues, a one-card reading can be expanded into a series of one-card readings. In that case, the querent and the Tarot reader engage in a dialogue that is facilitated by an occasional draw of a new card. Each card that is dealt examines the question just asked until a new question arises. This iterative process continues until all the querent's concerns have been addressed (or until the reading runs out of time). As an example, consider the following excerpt from this kind of conversational reading:

Querent: My boyfriend and I are having problems. He gets jealous easily, which makes me mad. How can I deal with this problem better?

The Nine of Cups is dealt.

KnightHawk: This card says that there is a lot that you can be satisfied about within this relationship. Try to focus on those good things and keep them in mind when your boyfriend gets jealous. In fact, just greeting his suspicions with happiness instead of anger might go a long way toward defusing his jealousy.

Q: Yeah, okay, but I don't deserve this treatment. I haven't done anything to make him jealous. How can I make him understand that?

The Queen of Wands reversed is dealt.

KH: The Queen of Wands is cheerful, and she radiates joy. However, since she is reversed here, I see her energy turning inward. Therefore, rather than trying to change your boyfriend's opinions, you should work on finding joy and happiness within yourself. Maybe changing yourself in this way will indirectly affect your boyfriend's perception of you. Even if it doesn't, such a change will help you stop feeling that your happiness is dependent on his good opinion of you, which will make you better able to deal with his jealousy.

Q: Hmmm. Maybe. But how do I do that? How can I make myself happier?

The Ace of Cups is dealt.

KH: I see a couple of things in this card. First, it says that you need to find a purer form of love in this relationship, such as trying to love your boyfriend for who he is rather than judge him for what he does wrong. Also, inasmuch as the Ace of Cups can be about idealized or higher forms of love—such as love for all mankind or divine love—it suggests that you pursue your spiritual path further in order to find more peace and serenity in your life.

This reading continued further, but this extract should be enough to illustrate the technique.

In a similar technique, the cards can facilitate a monologue instead of a dialogue. In this case, the querent poses a question and the Tarot reader deals one card, which begins to provide an answer. The reader finds as much insight in the card as she can, then deals another card, which may add to the message of the prior card, tackle the question from a new perspective, or move on to a related topic. Again, this process continues until the question has been answered or until time runs out.

The methods described above are some atypical techniques for reading the cards that I have found useful from time to time. Although rules (such as the ones we find in the definitions of spreads and instructions about how to read the cards) may be valuable for guiding and instructing the novice, once we learn and master those rules, it is okay to break them sometimes and to create our own rules. After all, reading Tarot cards is a living art, and our use of the cards is an evolutionary process that fosters and encourages the growth and development of that art.

So I encourage you to experiment with using the cards in daring, new ways. Be inventive. Listen to your intuition, and create your own spreads. But also, every once in a while, try to find entirely new ways of working with the cards that suit your needs, your temperament, and your style. Not only will you grow in the process, but so will the Tarot.

Bibliography and Recommended Reading

Tarot

Bunning, Joan. *Learning the Tarot*. York Beach, ME: Samuel Weiser, Inc., 1998.

Fairfield, Gail. *Choice-Centered Tarot*. York Beach, ME: Samuel Weiser, Inc., 1997.

Genetti, Alexandra. *Wheel of Change Tarot*. Rochester, VT: Destiny Books, 1997.

Greer, Mary K. *The Complete Book of Tarot Reversals*. St. Paul, MN: Llewellyn Publications, 2002.

———. *Tarot for Your Self*. North Hollywood, CA: Newcastle Publishing Co., 1984.

———. *Tarot Mirrors*. North Hollywood, CA: Newcastle Publishing Co., 1988.

Guiley, Rosemary Ellen, and Robert M. Place. *The Alchemical Tarot*. London: HarperCollins Publishers Ltd., 1995.

Kliegman, Isabel Radow. *Tarot and the Tree of Life*. Wheaton, IL: Quest Books, 1997.

Pollack, Rachel. *The Forest of Souls*. St. Paul, MN: Llewellyn Publications, 2002.

———. *Seventy-eight Degrees of Wisdom*. London: HarperCollins Publishers Ltd., 1997.

Ricklef, James. *Tarot Tells the Tale*. St. Paul, MN: Llewellyn Publications, 2003.

Rosengarten, Arthur. *Tarot and Psychology*. St. Paul, MN: Paragon House, 2000.

Thomson, Sandra A., Robert E. Mueller, and Signe E. Echols. *The Heart of the Tarot*. San Francisco: HarperSanFrancisco, 2000.

Waite, A. E. *The Pictorial Key to the Tarot*. 1910. Reprint, Stamford, CT: U.S. Games, 1990.

Qabalah

DuQuette, Lon Milo. *The Chicken Qabalah of Rabbi Lamed Ben Clifford.* York Beach, ME: Weiser Books, 2001.

Fortune, Dion. *The Mystical Qabalah.* London: Williams and Norgate, Ltd., 1935. Reprint, York Beach, ME: Samuel Weiser, Inc., 2000.

Wang, Robert. *The Qabalistic Tarot.* York Beach, ME: Samuel Weiser, Inc., 1983.

http://golden-dawn.org/qbl_gd.html

http://www.geocities.com/Athens/Troy/2795/index.html

http://kabbalah-web.org

Note that website addresses change frequently. If you find that a site is no longer available, you may want to try doing an Internet search (using, for example, Yahoo, Alta Vista, etc.) using keywords such as *Kabbalah* or *Qabalah.*

Fiction and Biographies

Barrie, J. M. *Peter Pan.* New York: Charles Scribner's Sons, 1980. First published 1911 under the title *Peter and Wendy.*

Brontë, Emily. *Wuthering Heights.* 1847. Reprint, New York: Random House, 1944.

Dickens, Charles. *A Christmas Carol.* 1843. Reprint, New York: Barnes & Noble, Inc., 1994.

Erickson, Carolly. *To the Scaffold: The Life of Marie Antoinette.* New York: W. Morrow and Co., 1991.

Goethe, Johann Wolfgang von. *Faust.* 1808–1832. Reprint, translated by Bayard Taylor. New York: Washington Square Press, Inc., 1964.

Homer. *The Odyssey.* Translated by Samuel Butler. New York: Barnes & Noble, Inc., 1993.

Mossiker, Frances. *Pocahontas: The Life and the Legend.* New York: Alfred A. Knopf, Inc., 1976.

Poe, Edgar Allan. *The Fall of the House of Usher and Other Writings.* 1839. Reprint, London: Penguin Books, Ltd., 1986.

Shakespeare, William. *The Taming of the Shrew.* Edited by Louis B. Wright and Virginia A. LaMar. New York: Simon & Schuster, 1963.

Singer, Armand. *A Bibliography of the Don Juan Theme.* Morgantown, WV: University of West Virginia Press, 1954.

Stapleton, Michael. *A Dictionary of Greek and Roman Mythology.* New York: Bell Publishing Co., 1978.

Wayne, Jane Ellen. *Clark Gable: Portrait of a Misfit.* New York: St. Martin's Press, 1993.

Wilde, Oscar. *The Picture of Dorian Gray and Other Writings.* 1891. Reprint, New York: Bantam Books, 1982.

———. *The Picture of Dorian Gray.* 1891. Reprint, New York: Random House, Modern Library, 1998.

LLEWELLYN ORDERING INFORMATION

Order Online:
Visit our website at www.llewellyn.com, select your books, and order them on our secure server.

Order by Phone:
- Call toll-free within the U.S. at 1-877-NEW-WRLD (1-877-639-9753). Call toll-free within Canada at 1-866-NEW-WRLD (1-866-639-9753)
- We accept VISA, MasterCard, and American Express

Order by Mail:
Send the full price of your order (MN residents add 7% sales tax) in U.S. funds, plus postage & handling to:

Llewellyn Worldwide
P.O. Box 64383, Dept. 0-7387-0345-1
St. Paul, MN 55164-0383, U.S.A.

Postage & Handling:

Standard (U.S., Mexico, & Canada). If your order is:
  $49.99 and under, add $3.00
  $50.00 and over, FREE STANDARD SHIPPING

AK, HI, PR: $15.00 for one book plus $1.00 for each additional book.

International Orders (airmail only):
  $16.00 for one book plus $3.00 for each additional book

Orders are processed within 2 business days. Please allow for normal shipping time.
Postage and handling rates subject to change.

Tarot Tells the Tale

*Explore Three-Card Readings
Through Familiar Stories*

JAMES RICKLEF

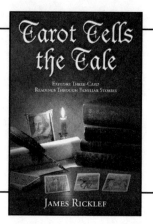

Through familiar stories learn nuances of reading Tarot that will help you answer any question. What if Scarlett O'Hara came to you for a Tarot reading, asking if Rhett was coming back to her? Or, if Abraham Lincoln wanted insight into the Civil War?

Peer over the shoulder of a Tarot master as he demonstrates the art of using three-card spreads to answer a variety of client questions. Through sample readings for famous characters from history, myth, and fiction, you will discover different ways to interpret personal cards, read reversed cards, construct a good question, and even rephrase less-than-ideal questions. Explore the many permutations of the basic three-card spread, as well as how to break the common Celtic Cross into minispreads. As a result, you will find that your readings will become more synthesized, cohesive, and coherent.

0-7387-0272-2
288 pp., 6 x 9, illus.   **$16.95**

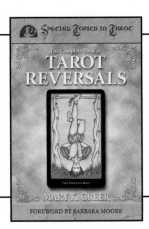

The Complete Book of Tarot Reversals

Mary K. Greer

What do you do with the "other half" of a Tarot reading: the reversed cards? Just ignore them as many people do? *The Complete Book of Tarot Reversals* reveals everything you need to know for reading the most maligned and misunderstood part of a spread. These interpretations offer inner support, positive advice, and descriptions of the learning opportunities available, yet with a twist that is uniquely their own.

Enhance and deepen the quality of your consultations as you experiment with the eleven different methods of reading reversed cards. Use the author's interpretations to stimulate your own intuitive ideas. Struggle in the dark no longer.

1-56718-285-2
288 pp., 6 x 9, illus.   **$14.95**

To Write to the Author

If you wish to contact the author or would like more information about this book, please write to the author in care of Llewellyn Worldwide and we will forward your request. Both the author and publisher appreciate hearing from you and learning of your enjoyment of this book and how it has helped you. Llewellyn Worldwide cannot guarantee that every letter written to the author can be answered, but all will be forwarded. Please write to:

James Ricklef
% Llewellyn Worldwide
P.O. Box 64383, Dept. 0-7387-0345-1
St. Paul, MN 55164-0383, U.S.A.
Please enclose a self-addressed stamped envelope for reply,
or $1.00 to cover costs. If outside U.S.A., enclose
international postal reply coupon.

Many of Llewellyn's authors have websites with additional information and resources. For more information, please visit our website at http://www.llewellyn.com.